France since the Second World War

SEMINAR STUDIES   IN HISTORY

France since the Second World War

TYLER E. STOVALL

An imprint of **Pearson Education**

Harlow, England · London · New York · San Francisco · Toronto · Don Mills, Ontario · Sydney · Tokyo
Singapore · Hong Kong · Seoul · Taipei · Cape Town · Madrid · Mexico City · Amsterdam · Munich · Paris · Milan

PEARSON EDUCATION LIMITED

Head Office:
Edinburgh Gate
Harlow
Essex CM20 2JE
Tel: +44 (0)1279 623623
Fax +44 (0)1279 431059

London Office:
128 Long Acre
London WC2E 9AN
Tel: +44 (0)20 7447 2000
Fax: +44 (0)20 7240 5771
Website: www.history-minds.com

First published in Great Britain in 2002

© Pearson Education Limited 2002

The right of Tyler E. Stovall to be identified as author
of this work has been asserted by him in accordance
with the Copyright, Designs and Patents Act 1988.

ISBN 0 582 36882 0

British Library Cataloguing-in-Publication Data
A CIP catalogue record for this book can be obtained from the British Library

10 9 8 7 6 5 4 3 2 1

Typeset by 7 in 10/12 Sabon Roman
Printed in Malaysia, LSP

The Publishers' policy is to use paper manufactured from sustainable forests.

For Justin
To whom the twentieth century is only history

CONTENTS

INTRODUCTION TO THE SERIES

Such is the pace of historical enquiry in the modern world that there is an ever-widening gap between the specialist article or monograph, incorporating the results of current research, and general surveys, which inevitably become out of date. *Seminar Studies in History* is designed to bridge this gap. The series was founded by Patrick Richardson in 1966 and his aim was to cover major themes in British, European and World history. Between 1980 and 1996 Roger Lockyer continued his work, before handing the editorship over to Clive Emsley and Gordon Martel. Clive Emsley is Professor of History at the Open University, while Gordon Martel is Professor of International History at the University of Northern British Columbia, Canada, and Senior Research Fellow at De Montfort University.

All the books are written by experts in their field who are not only familiar with the latest research but have often contributed to it. They are frequently revised, in order to take account of new information and interpretations. They provide a selection of documents to illustrate major themes and provoke discussion, and also a guide to further reading. The aim of *Seminar Studies in History* is to clarify complex issues without over-simplifying them, and to stimulate readers into deepening their knowledge and understanding of major themes and topics.

LIST OF ABBREVIATIONS

CGT	General Confederation of Labour
CNRS	National Council for Scientific Research
DOM-TOMs	Overseas departments and territories
EEC	European Economic Community
EMU	European Monetary Union
ENA	National Administration School
FEN	National Union of Higher Education
FLN	National Liberation Front (Algeria)
HLM	*Habitations à loyer modéré*
INSEE	National Institute of Statistical Studies
MRP	People's Republican Movement
OAS	Secret Army Organisation (Algeria)
PCF	French Communist Party
PS	French Socialist Party (post-1971)
RPF	Rally of the French People
SFIO	French Socialist Party (pre-1971)
SNE-Sup	Union of Teachers in Higher Education
SNES	National Union of Secondary School Teachers
UDF	French Democratic Union
UDSR	Democratic and Socialist Union of Resistance
UNEF	National Union of French Students

AUTHOR'S ACKNOWLEDGEMENTS

A number of individuals deserve my most sincere appreciation for helping me write this book. I am very grateful to Gordon Martel, editor of the *Seminar Studies in History* at Pearson Education, for initially suggesting this project to me, and patiently seeing it through to completion. Emily Pillars and Sarah Bury helped turn a rough manuscript into a polished piece of work. My colleague Alan S. Christy carefully read the entire manuscript, taking valuable time away from his own work, and my friends W. Scott Haine and Robert Frost also lent their expertise to this project. I would also like to thank Mike Vann and Robin Mitchell for their support and helpful suggestions. It is of course understood that any errors in this text remain the sole responsibility of the author. I am very appreciative of the funding support given by the department of History and by the division of the Humanities at the University of California, Santa Cruz. Finally, my thanks go to my wife, Denise Herd, and son, Justin Stovall, for their support, understanding and especially patience.

PUBLISHER'S ACKNOWLEDGEMENTS

We are grateful to the following for permission to reproduce copyright material:

Editions du Seuil, Paris (Documents 1–3, 10, 18). Harcourt, Brace and Co., New York (Document 4). Beacon Press, Boston (Document 5, 13, 14). Vintage, New York (Document 6). Gallimand, Paris (Document 7). Yale Southeast Asia Centre, New Haven (Document 8). Alfred A. Knopf, New York (Document 9). David Godine, Boston (Document 11). Atheneum, New York (Document 12). Harper and Row, New York (Document 15). Fayard, Paris (Document 16). Harvard University Press (Document 17). *Le Monde* (Document 19)

Agence Roger Viollet (Plates 1–7).
Earl and Donna Evleth (Plates 8–10).

In some instances we have been unable to trace the owners of copyright material and we would appreciate any information which would enable us to do so.

CHRONOLOGY

1944

25 August — Liberation of Paris

September — Charles de Gaulle appointed head of Provisional Government

1945

May — Defeat of Nazi Germany and end of the Second World War

Sétif massacre in Algeria

October — Legislative elections

Founding of journal *Les Temps Modernes*

1946

January — De Gaulle resigns as head of government

May — Constitutional referendum

October — A second constitutional referendum approves the Fourth Republic

November — Bombardment of Haiphong, start of the Indochina war

1947

April–May — French Communist Party (PCF) quits government, massive strikes, the end of Tripartism

Start of the first Five Year Plan

Feud over 'Coca-colonization'

Uprising in Madagascar against French rule

1948

October–November — Major coal mining strikes confirm the political isolation of the PCF

1949 — Simone de Beauvoir publishes *The Second Sex*

Communist victory in China improves fortunes of Viet Minh in the war against France

1950 — Founding of Club Med

1952	Albert Camus publishes *The Rebel*
	Start of the second Five Year Plan
1954	
May	Battle of Dien Bien Phu, end of the war in Indochina
November	Beginning of the Algerian war
1955	
June	Phillippeville massacre in Algeria, escalation of the French war effort
1956	Morocco and Tunisia achieve independence from France
	Battle of Algiers
	Sartre and other Parisian intellectuals denounce the Soviet invasion of Hungary
1958	
May–June	Settlers' uprising in Algiers, collapse of the Fourth Republic
	De Gaulle returns to power, founding of the Fifth Republic
September	Referendum in the colonies on membership in the new French Community
	Claude Lévi-Strauss publishes *Structural Anthropology*
1959	Birth of New Wave school of cinema, with films by Claude Chabrol, Alain Resnais, and François Truffaut
1960	Secret Army Organisation (OAS) founded in Algeria
	France grants independence to fourteen black African colonies
	Albert Camus dies in a car crash
1962	France grants Algerian independence
1964	Founding of the University of Paris campus at Nanterre
1967	Birth of student New Left at Nanterre
1968	
May–June	May 1968 movement, massive strikes by students and workers

1968	De Gaulle resigns after losing a popular referendum; Pompidou becomes president
1970	Death of Charles de Gaulle
1971	Epinay congress of the Socialist Party; Mitterrand becomes party leader
	Opening of the documentary *The Sorrow and the Pity*
1972	The Socialist Party (PS) and PCF establish Common Programme
	Founding of the National Front
1973	World oil crisis, end of postwar prosperity
1974	Giscard-d'Estaing elected president
	Solzhenitsyn's *Gulag Archipelago* published in French translation
1981	Mitterrand elected president of France. PS takes control of the Legislature
1982	Mitterrand administration drops Keynesian economic policies, embraces deflationary position to cope with the recession
1984	National Front wins 11 per cent of the vote in elections to the European Parliament
1985	France signs Schengen Agreement with West Germany and the Low Countries
1986	PS loses legislative elections, leading to two years of 'cohabitation', with Mitterrand as president, Gaullist leader Jacques Chirac as prime minister
1987	Trial of Klaus Barbie for war crimes
1988	Mitterrand re-elected president

1991	Revelation of HIV-contaminated blood scandal
1992	France ratifies the Maastricht agreement Birth of the European Monetary Union
1995	Jacques Chirac elected president of France
1996	Death of François Mitterrand
1997	Election of Socialist leader Lionel Jospin as Prime Minister
1998	France's victory in the World Cup Trial and conviction of Maurice Papon
1999	Split of the National Front into two factions Introduction of the Eurodollar
2000	France and the world celebrate the dawn of a new millennium

PART ONE   BACKGROUND

CHAPTER ONE

INTRODUCTION

At first glance, the history of France over the last half-century seems like a straightforward affair. Compared to the previous fifty years, an era dominated by two world wars and a massive economic depression between, the French seem to have been living in relatively quiet times since 1945. Yet such a perspective soon disappears once one bothers to look below the surface. Recent French history has been a period of important changes, of triumphs in overcoming old problems and of the rise of new issues for the nation. The last fifty-five years have fundamentally transformed life in France, so much so that a French woman or man in 1940 would probably have more in common with a similar individual in 1880 than one in 1970. At the same time the recent era has dramatically altered the position of France in the wider world. Only recently recognised as one of the world's great powers, France began this period as a recently liberated nation, then had to search for an independent role in a Europe starkly divided between capitalism and Communism. The last decade has brought further uncertainties for the nation with both the end of the Cold War and the accelerated push for European unification. The relationship between France and its overseas colonies has also transformed the country's global impact, as formal empire gave way to neo-colonialism abroad and a new multiculturalism at home. Therefore, not only have the last fifty-five years witnessed numerous exciting (and sometimes tragic) events, they have also brought about reassessments of the very nature of French identity. The question 'what does it mean to be French?' that has been so central to national life since the Revolution of 1789, re-emerged with particular acuity during the late twentieth century.

Writing the history of such a recent period offers both problems and opportunities. In general, historians are used to the study of eras much further removed from our own, eras which are sufficiently distant to allow the development of some perspective and, perhaps (although certainly not always), objectivity. One can then take advantage of government documents, memoirs, and other sources that may not be available for some time until after the deaths of their authors. This is especially true in France, whose ancient national tradition has meant that the Revolution of 1789 counts as 'modern' history. Indeed, many French scholars would hesitate to consider the chronicle of the late twentieth century 'history' at all. As a result, compared to other eras the historiography of France since 1945 is definitely underdeveloped. In comparison to the historiography of the nineteenth century, or even of the Second World War, there have been few major disputes between historians, or reassessments of historical ideas once taken for granted (the studies of intellectual life in the age of existentialism, and of decolonisation, provide exceptions to this general rule). However, it is also true that the newness of the period provides important advantages. Not only is source material, in the form of books, newspaper and journal articles, and government documents far more abundant, but one can also take advantage of scholarship in fields like political science, sociology and anthropology. Perhaps most useful is the fact that many people who lived through the era are still alive and can furnish direct testimony about their own experiences and that of France in general. The scholar or student who writes about the history of France since 1945 thus situates him or herself at the beginning of an historiographical tradition.

While this era of French history is thus a surprisingly diverse and complex one, a few themes stand out. Certainly the interaction between France and the broader world, especially in the context of Cold War and decolonisation, is an important one. Also central to the French experience since the Second World War is economic prosperity and modernisation, as well as the impact of recession after the mid-1970s. However, if there is one issue that can best serve as a mirror for the general history of France since 1945, it is the changing legacy of the war and, more particularly, of the Resistance against Nazism and Vichy. The Second World War traumatised the French people, bringing not only death and destruction on a massive scale but also the first fully-fledged foreign occupation in well over a century. During the most somber days of the Vichy era the French had to look deep into their souls, pondering in what form France would survive, or even would it survive at all. It was the Resistance, both the Free French led by Charles de Gaulle and the guerrilla fighters operating clandestinely within occupied France, that answered this question, affirming the continuity and renewal of French nationhood and identity. The significance of the Resistance was much more emotional and psychological than military, for while it did not defeat Nazism, it did salvage French honour, enabling the French to claim they had rejected fascism. Moreover, the Resistance was not just a struggle against German occupation but also a powerful movement for social justice and the creation of a new, more egalitarian society. Those who fought its battles wanted to make France great not by simply rebuilding the old society, but rather by creating a new, happier and more just France, one in which fascism would have no place.

During the last half of the twentieth century the spirit of the Resistance provided a general guideline to many important aspects of French national life. One could only succeed in many spheres of postwar French society if one had the right Resistance credentials. More generally, the experience of the struggle against fascism served as a blueprint for the creation of a new France, as well as a litmus test for the success or failure of that project. In some important ways, notably economic modernisation and social planning, France successfully used the legacy of the Resistance to guide the restoration and development of the nation after 1945. In others, such as political life and colonial policy, the influence of ideas derived from the Resistance played a less positive role. For good or ill, during the thirty years after the end of the Second World War the spirit of the anti-fascist struggle formed a crucial definition of what it meant to be French. In contrast, during the last two decades of the twentieth century many in France began questioning aspects of the Resistance legacy, and the wartime experience gradually lost its hold over national life. This process of redefinition served ultimately to move France out of the postwar era into a new, turn-of-the-century phase of its history. By the 1990s the French were dealing with a new series of problems and challenges, unanticipated in 1945, that suggested the hazy outlines of an as yet undetermined future.

*   *   *

Given that the events of the Second World War played such a powerful role in determining the history of postwar France, it makes sense to provide a brief overview of that era, and the early twentieth century in general. In contrast to the dynamism of French society after 1945, France during the years from 1900 to 1944 seemed to many observers stagnant and adrift, without a firm national mission or sense of the future. Although universally recognised as a great power in Europe and overseas, with the second-largest colonial empire in the world, early twentieth-century France lacked the drive and excitement that so characterised the eras of Louis XIV, the Revolution of 1789, and Napoleon. In terms of government the nation was ruled by the regime known as the Third Republic, created in 1870 after the defeat of the Franco-Prussian war. The Third Republic deserves credit for making the ideal of France as a secular democratic republic, an ideal born in the Revolution, a reality. It fought off numerous challenges by right-wing groups in the Army and the Catholic Church to republicanism, in the process sowing its ideals and institutions in every city, town and village in the country. It also presided over major changes in French society, as the advent of modern manufacturing began the transformation of France into an industrialised nation, and created a vast new French empire in Africa and Southeast Asia.

By the beginning of the twentieth century, however, the Third Republic seemed to have lost much of its vigour. After surviving the latest and greatest challenge from the Right, the Dreyfus Affair, the broad liberal coalition that had defended the Republic began to drift apart. New social and political challenges emerged, especially the ever more violent conflicts between industrialists and French workers. At the same time international relations in Europe, especially tensions between France and the new German empire, became more and more difficult. In August 1914, these tensions led Germany to invade France, shattering nearly a century of peace in Europe and initiating the First World War. With the aid of its allies, Britain and especially the United States, France eventually won the war after over four years of shocking carnage, but the cost was very high: 1.3 million French men, one out of every ten adult males in the country, died in the war. More generally, the prospect of such dreadful slaughter after a century of progress and confidence in the superiority of European civilisation, shook the confidence of many in the nation's prospects for the future. In particular, while Germany was defeated, it remained larger and potentially stronger than France; moreover, many Germans were now embittered by their loss of the war, and thirsted for revenge against the French. France may have won the war, but a secure peace remained an illusive dream.

During the 1920s France seemed to recover from the damage inflicted by war, so that by the end of the decade the economy was more prosperous than ever. The literary and artistic avant-garde flourished, usually criticising nineteenth-century conventions and exploring the psychological and irrational dimensions of human existence. France became more than ever a world centre, so that no nation received more foreign immigrants during the decade. Paris in particular played host to a dazzling array of foreign artists, from Pablo Picasso to Ernest Hemingway. Yet much of the interwar years was dominated by a futile attempt to return to the vanished certainties of the prewar era. France was one of the very few European nations to refuse the vote to women after the war, preferring to emphasise their role as mothers in order to boost the birth rate. The postwar prosperity generally did not reach the country's working class, whose discontent was increasingly voiced by the small but vocal Communist Party. Such discontent increased markedly with the onset of the great Depression, a worldwide economic crisis which struck France in 1931. The crisis impoverished many farmers and threw hundreds of thousands of labourers out of work. It also revealed the instability of the Third Republic, as government after government showed itself incapable of restoring economic health. Depression gave rise to political and international tensions, as the Nazi seizure of power in Germany helped spawn fascist movements all over Europe, including in France itself. The mid-1930s saw those French people opposed to fascism rally into a broad left-wing alliance known as the Popular Front, which won the elections of 1936 and installed Léon Blum as the nation's first Socialist (and Jewish) prime minister. Begun with high hopes, the Blum government soon foundered on the reefs of continued economic crisis as well as discord between its Radical and Communist coalition partners, collapsing entirely in 1938.

When the Second World War began in September 1939, therefore, France was a nation bitterly divided by politics and still economically weak. Although in the late 1930s French governments had begun feverish policies of rearmament, the nation lagged noticeably behind the military might of Nazi Germany. Nonetheless, the rapidity and completeness of France's defeat by Germany in May and June of 1940 came as a horrible shock to most French people. For the next four years the nation was occupied by Nazi soldiers, and ruled by a collaborationist government set up by the French themselves in the resort town of Vichy. Vichy represented not just a desire to appease the Germans, but also important sectors of the French far Right, which thirsted for revenge against the Popular Front and liberal republicanism in general. Many French people collaborated more or less actively with the Vichy regime during the Occupation, their motivations ranging from weary resignation to an enthusiastic embrace. But others rejected Vichy and Nazism, choosing the path of resistance. In June of 1940, Charles de Gaulle, then the youngest general in the French Army, broadcast a radio appeal from London for continued resistance, and thereafter moved to set up the Free French forces, proclaiming himself the legitimate head in exile of the French nation. At the same time resistance groups began forming in occupied France itself, gradually growing to the scale of fully-fledged guerrilla armies. When Nazi Germany invaded the Soviet Union in 1941, the French Communist Party leaped headlong into resistance activity, soon becoming a leading force in the movement. The action of the PCF symbolised a broader characteristic of the Resistance as a left-wing movement, the wartime continuation of the anti-fascist tradition represented by the Popular Front. As the military fortunes of the Germans began to decline, so did French support for Vichy, while more and more embraced the alternative represented by de Gaulle and the guerrillas. The D-Day landings in June 1944 spelled the end of the Occupation of France, and by August Allied soldiers, led by the Free French themselves, liberated the nation's capital. Anti-fascism had triumphed in France, and now pressed for a profound, even revolutionary, renewal of the nation.

It is at this point that our story begins.

PART TWO   ANALYSIS

CHAPTER TWO

LIBERATION AND RENEWAL

For France, as for most of the world, 1945 was a year of choices, of roads taken and not taken. For six years the nation had been locked in conflict with Nazi Germany, years dominated by humiliating defeat and brutal military occupation. In 1945 this nightmare finally came to an end, and the French nation emerged victorious from one of the greatest struggles of its history. Yet in 1945 France may have won the war, but the nature of the peace remained to be determined. The success of the war against Nazism had for the foreseeable future foreclosed one model of French society, that represented by the Vichy state. At the same time, few wanted to return to the stratified society and inept politics of the Third Republic, widely blamed for the paralysis of the nation in the face of economic crisis and the threat of fascism during the 1930s. While the Second World War had undermined the viability of some perspectives on French society, it had at the same time created others that attracted supporters among different political groups in the nation. From the aging but triumphant Stalinism of the Soviet Union to the capitalist democracy of the United States, France regarded a myriad of paths into the second half of the century.

In the six years after the death of Adolf Hitler, France did make its choice, opting to recreate a system of bourgeois parliamentary democracy. The new political structures of postwar France resembled those of the prewar era to a striking extent, so that to some the Fourth Republic seemed like a spiffed-up version of the Third. This was a remarkable outcome, since the immediate postwar period had been dominated by voices calling for the creation of a new France, one that would avoid all the mistakes and tragedies of the old. In particular, it involved the marginalisation of the two most powerful political forces in the country at the Liberation: Charles de Gaulle and the French Communist Party (PCF). Refusing the choice between Caesar and Lenin, the French instead reaffirmed their preference for a form of government, the parliamentary Republic, whose roots lay deep in French history and constituted an important Gallic contribution to Western civilisation. France also rejected the bleak Manichaeanism of the emerging

Cold War between the United States and the Soviet Union. While France quickly found its way into the American camp after 1945, it retained a significant amount of independence in the relationship, pursuing ties with the world's greatest superpower for its own reasons rather than simply in response to Yankee military and economic supremacy. Nor did France completely cut its ties with the Russians, whose perspectives on colonialism, German rearmament, and other questions continued to win support far beyond the faithful ranks of the PCF. Ultimately, in the decade after the war France chose to become neither the USA nor the USSR, but instead to remain France.

This chapter will tell the story of how and why the French people made this choice, and demonstrate that this choice determined the basic outlines of national life in the latter half of the twentieth century. However, the decision to restore bourgeois parliamentary democracy in France did not mean a flight into nostalgia or a doomed attempt to restore the past. Rather, the first decade of the postwar era represents an example of new wine in old bottles; whereas the new political structures of the Fourth Republic may have had a familiar ring about them, they brought into being a radically new and distinct French society.

FRANCE IN 1945

In the year of Nazi Germany's capitulation France stood firmly on the side of the winning powers, yet in its material poverty and political uncertainty looked more like one of the losers. Compared to eastern and central Europe, or even Britain, the nation was fortunate; it had suffered neither widespread bombings nor prolonged military campaigns on most of its soil. But economic activity had practically come to a standstill in 1945. Industrial production that year was less than 40 per cent of 1938 levels; in the crucial coal mining sector it was only 20 per cent. Much of the nation's transportation infrastructure, notably many ports, railroads and bridges, had been put out of action by the fighting during the Liberation. In consequence, while some areas were full of food (notably Normandy, where farmers stacked up pyramids of Camembert cheese they were unable to sell), others, especially urban areas, experienced levels of hunger as bad or worse than during the years of the Occupation. The winter of 1944/45 was an extremely harsh one, made all the worse by major coal shortages. Infant mortality increased, and doctors estimated that three-quarters of French city-dwellers were clinically malnourished. Two million houses had been severely damaged or destroyed, and a million families had no homes. Above all, the weakness of the French franc and the shortages of food and other basic commodities produced runaway inflation, as prices raced ahead of wages in the immediate postwar years. The stubborn refusal of France's economic problems to fade away in the bright light of victory sharpened their impact: during the most sombre years of the Occupation many had come to believe that with the Liberation they would once again have enough decent food to eat and fuel to heat their homes. Yet in 1945 peace had been achieved but its fruits remained tantalisingly out of reach (Werth, 1956).

A number of factors made economic recovery difficult immediately after the war. Obviously, the devastation caused by the war itself would take some time to repair. Fuel shortages and transportation blockages limited the ability of key industries to boost production, as did labour shortages, most notably the slow return of over two million French prisoners of war and concentration camp inmates from Germany. These problems hurt agricultural output in particular: thanks to inadequate numbers of farm workers, fertilisers and agricultural machinery during the war, by 1945 wheat, potato and wine crops were down some 25 to 40 per cent in comparison to prewar levels. Industrial and agricultural shortages forced France to import crucial materials, leading to a huge balance of payments deficit which exerted steady downward pressure on the franc. In short, the crisis of production in the postwar period meant there was little to consume: in order to eat more, the French would have to make more.

Worst of all, not everyone shared the postwar privations to the same degree. Many anti-fascist French, especially those involved in the Resistance, had viewed fascism as not just political and military dictatorship, but also as the ultimate example of social inequality. The victory over the Nazis and the French collaborators was supposed to bring about a more just society, one in which the wealthy could no longer flaunt their riches while others suffered. In order to share the nation's material burdens as equitably as possible, for example, political authorities after the Liberation retained food and fuel rationing and price controls. The result, however, was a flourishing black market, especially for food, where those who could pay its sky-high prices could obtain whatever they wanted, thus reducing the amounts available at the official cost. Particularly vexing was the belief, shared by many, that the so-called 'economic collaborators' of the war years had emerged from the Liberation unscathed by justice to enjoy the illegitimate fruits of the black market while patriotic and honest French families had to do without. As Janet Flanner noted in March 1945, 'The last time the French around here had butter was Christmas Eve. The food situation is frightful. ...The French realize that the black-market butter, even if diverted to legal channels, would not spread one slice of bread per citizen per day, but what they want, and quickly, is some symbolic act of justice, invention, efficacy, and administrative gumption. Butter has taken on political qualities' (Flanner, 1965: 20).

In fact, everything seemed to have 'taken on political qualities' in

France just after the Liberation. The nation trembled on the edge of revolution; never before or since in the twentieth century would capitalism be in such danger. Challenges to the *status quo* varied widely. At the most local level food and fuel riots proliferated; in January 1,200 people invaded and looted a coal mine near Lille, while in March 5,000 Parisian house-wives staged an 'anti-hunger' demonstration outside City Hall. Summary executions of suspected collaborators continued during the early months of 1945, although their number was far less than that suggested by right-wing paranoia. More significantly, the French Communist Party emerged from the war with enhanced prestige as the *parti des fusillés* (the party of martyrs), not to mention hundreds of thousands of new members and a large, only recently demobilised partisan army. The October elections for the Constituent Assembly made the PCF the largest political party in the country. Overall, the Liberation represented not just the defeat of Nazi Germany but equally the triumph of the Left over the Right. The Resistance vision of a France renewed was profoundly political, and the word 'socialism' summed up for many French women and men their hopes for a better day.

In general, if 1944 had brought the explosion of joy and relief that greeted the end of the Occupation, 1945 manifested a more sombre spirit of reflection over what had been lost, and reckoning with an uncertain future. One of the year's most poignant and disturbing phenomena was the gradual return of French prisoners of war and, most tragically, concentration camp inmates from defeated Germany. The terrible physical condition and fre-quent mental disorientation of these unfortunates not only graphically demonstrated the depths of Nazi iniquity, but also drove home the point that the heart of the war had been boundless human suffering rather than military or political combat. The persistence of prewar political conflicts and wartime deprivation made it clear that the defeat of Nazism had not solved France's problems, but only given her new opportunities to engage them. In such a climate of disenchantment the bleak 'existentialist' phil-osophies of Jean-Paul Sartre, Albert Camus and others resonated far beyond the picturesque streets of Saint-Germain-des-Prés. Humanity was condemned to struggle for freedom, and even victory did not necessarily bring happiness. 1945 also brought the new presence of the Soviet Union and the United States as superpowers, symbolised by the spectre of the Red Flag over Berlin's ruined Reichstag in May, and America's nuclear oblit-eration of Hiroshima and Nagasaki in August. In such a radically changed world, what would be the place of France? In 1945, at least, few could offer a definitive answer to this agonising question.

POLITICAL RENEWAL

On 25 August 1944, the day Paris was liberated, Charles de Gaulle strode down the Champs Elysées at the head of a million rejoicing French men and women who received him with the kind of welcome usually reserved for kings and prophets. Some sixteen months later, on 20 January 1946, he resigned as head of the French government, a position he would not regain for over a decade. Like Britain, France in the immediate postwar years decided that the great wartime leader was not necessarily the best man to build the peace. De Gaulle's transition from national hero to political outcast most dramatically illustrates France's transition from Vichy to the Fourth Republic after the war. It was a turbulent period politically, in which many competing visions of a new nation clashed and French women and men proclaimed and re-evaluated the hopes born during the Occupation. Ironically, in an era in which everyone seemed to want renewal and change, the political result was a new republican government more similar to the supposedly discredited past than to the imagined future.

The domination of the Left constituted the central fact of French political life in the years immediately after the war. This represented a shift of the pendulum from the exaggerated right-wing dominance of Vichy to the equally exaggerated triumph of the Resistance. Although the Free French did not by themselves win the war, they stood for that part of France which had chosen the right side. One could only portray France as a nation of resisters, not collaborators, if one granted the Resistance a key leadership role; the political triumph of the Left thus arose out of not just military victory, but also a deeply-felt need to preserve national honour. Consequently, immediately after the war the voices of those on the Right were effectively silenced, lest they be accused of collaboration. Instead, the so-called Party of the Resistance held effective sway, so that only political forces and organisations who had played some role in the anti-fascist struggle could claim a share of power. However, as quickly became clear after the Liberation, the wartime practice of Resistance unity would not survive in the new era.

Of the various factions of the Resistance, the French Communist Party (PCF) appeared the most powerful in the postwar years. The party had undergone a remarkable transformation during the war, changing from a small, isolated left-wing sect to a national political party. The strength of the PCF, based on the leading role it played in the Resistance, led many observers to predict a revolution or Communist *coup d'état* in France, fears that became more concrete with the proliferation of Soviet satellites in Eastern Europe. Yet the PCF itself rejected the idea of revolution in the postwar years, in large part due to the hopes of the Soviet Union for continued cooperation with the West. Upon his return from his wartime exile in Moscow, PCF leader Maurice Thorez proclaimed the party's main goals to be the maintenance of wartime unity and victory in the 'Battle of Production'. In spite of this stated moderation, the broader political aims of the PCF remained unclear. The Socialist Party had also gained a new lease on life from its role in the Resistance, although it had been less active than the PCF. In consequence, it became, for the first time, the junior party of the far Left. The party was led, as before the war, by Léon Blum, the first Socialist prime minister of France who now returned in triumph from his wartime imprisonment by the Germans. Thanks to Blum and other Socialists who had not forgotten the bitter prewar conflicts with the PCF, attempts to merge France's two great collectivist parties came to naught after the Liberation.

More significant change took place in the parties of the old centre Left, now effectively the political Right in France. That classic organisation of the Third Republic, the Radical Party, also re-established itself after the war. However, its appeal seemed dated to many, and it would never regain its prewar prominence. Some political leaders, seeking to reconstitute the Centre as an advocate for the 'little man' against both the power of the big shots and the collectivist threat of the Communists created a new group, the Democratic and Socialist Union of the Resistance (UDSR), but their creation failed to make much impression on the electorate. Far more successful was the other new party of the Centre, the People's Republican Movement (MRP). The MRP represented a new, revived Christian Democracy, in which Catholicism at long last fully accepted the Republic and shared the general belief of other Resistance veterans in creating a more just society. Headed by Georges Bidault, former head of the National Resistance Council, the MRP's credentials were impeccable, yet it also firmly opposed the Marxism of the PCF. In consequence, the MRP's membership and electorate paradoxically began to attract conservatives, French men and women who rejected the beliefs of the Resistance and yet voted for the MRP as the best alternative to a real right-wing party. In the immediate postwar period attempts to unite these Centre-Left parties, with or without the Socialists, foundered amid suspicion and uncertainty. After 1948, in contrast, their general outlook would dominate the Fourth Republic.

And then there was Charles de Gaulle, the man above parties, who ruled France as a benevolent dictator for the first year after the Liberation. The tension between de Gaulle and the left-wing parties that would ultimately bring about the great leader's downfall had its roots in the wartime contrast between the Free French and the Resistance partisans. The former wished an orderly restoration of prewar France, with a much stronger leader; the latter fought for a more profound social transformation of French society. Those who had fought and suffered inside occupied France felt their sacrifices entitled them to the moral leadership of the nation. Many Gaullists felt, in contrast, that the Resistance only represented a minority, no matter how brave, of the French, whereas de Gaulle stood for the nation as a whole. Moreover, the aristocratic de Gaulle frequently viewed the working class, rag tag members of the Resistance with distaste and disdain. Lucie Aubrac, a leading member of the Resistance, described one incident that revealed the tensions between the two sides:

> ... on another occasion, at Lyon, he [de Gaulle] wanted to sit at a banquet between the Prefect and the *Commissaire de la République*. Instead, we put him between two leaders of the local Resistance. He took it very badly, looked like thunder, and didn't address one word to them throughout the meal. (Werth, 1956: 228)

In September 1944, de Gaulle appointed the official provisional government, charged with running the country until elections could be scheduled and a new permanent regime established. The majority of the government's members were followers of de Gaulle, although a large minority had served in the Resistance, including both Socialists and Communists. Differences between the two sides soon became manifest. The party leaders wished to pursue far-reaching socio-economic changes, and did push through the nationalisation of the coal mines, the Navy, the Renault auto company, and a few other key industrial sectors. The Gaullists displayed much less enthusiasm, feeling such reforms should await a clearer mandate from the electorate. De Gaulle's economic policy, notably his refusal to devalue the franc or institute strict currency controls, increased inflation and consequently caused a decline in working-class living standards. Resistance leaders at times accused the Gaullists of leniency towards former Vichyites during the purge trials of 1945, trials they wished would not only punish the guilty but also democratise France's administration by removing much of the old elite. As these disagreements festered, the political parties threw themselves into mobilising their supporters for the October 1945 legislative elections. These elections, the first national ones in nearly a decade, would elect a Constituent Assembly whose members would draw up the constitution for the new Republic.

The October elections were distinctive in several respects. Most significantly for the long term, they represented the first time in French history in which women voted, gaining a right which most of their sisters in Europe and America had acquired a generation earlier. With the establishment of women's suffrage France could at long last claim to be a fully-fledged democracy. The electoral results demonstrated graphically how far French opinion had shifted to the Left as a result of war and Liberation: three-quarters of all electors voted for the three main Resistance parties. The PCF won the largest share of the vote, 27 per cent, while the Socialists came in third with 24 per cent. France's two 'Marxist' parties could therefore claim a slender but absolute majority of the electorate. The new MRP won a quarter of the vote, in part due to rightist electors who supported it as the best of a bad lot. Throughout the campaign de Gaulle remained uncharacteristically silent, clinging to his image as a man above political parties who represented France as a whole. This fiction ended a few months later when de Gaulle suddenly resigned as leader of the Constituent Assembly, preferring to relinquish power rather than bow to the will of the parliamentary Left.

The elections revealed a massive desire for change, but as the new Assembly quickly demonstrated, they did not provide a consensus on how to achieve it, or specifically what kind of constitution would best suit the postwar era. One side, dominated by de Gaulle and his supporters, favoured a government with a strong executive. These individuals pointed to the Third Republic as a prime example of a weak executive in a parliamentary system, implying that its collapse and the rise of Vichy could have been prevented by a more powerful leader. The other side proposed a system with a strong Legislature, led by an Executive Committee. This was the old Jacobin model, and not surprisingly its main advocate was the PCF, now the strongest single party in the Constituent Assembly. Many in France had questions about both proposals and suspected the motives of de Gaulle and the PCF, viewing both as potentially anti-democratic. Nonetheless, after several months of acrimonious debate, the Constituent Assembly came up with a constitutional proposal that emphasised parliamentary control and provided a series of checks and balances on executive authority.

The MRP in particular led the campaign against the new constitution, claiming it heavily favoured the Communists, and voters rejected the proposal handily in a May 1946 referendum. This vote meant that the Constituent Assembly had to repeat the entire process of drafting a constitution all over again. A month later France held new legislative elections in which the MRP, flush with its recent successful campaign against the proposed constitution, now emerged as the largest political party. The MRP, working together with the third place Socialists, now took the lead in revising the constitutional draft. These revisions included the addition of more limitations on the executive branch of government, as well as revised structures for France's overseas colonies, renaming the empire the French Union. The Assembly completed its new draft by early summer, and scheduled a new referendum for October 1946. This time de Gaulle led the opposition to the proposed constitution. On 18 June he gave a speech advocating his so-called 'Bayeux Constitution', which would have set up a republic dominated by the president, and in subsequent speeches warned that France needed a strong state to maintain its place in a complex and hostile world. The subsequent electoral campaign reproduced all the previous tensions between de Gaulle and the three Resistance parties, and had the significant impact of bringing the former leader of Free France the allegiance of much of the right-wing electorate. The 13 October referendum produced a narrow victory, 9 million to 8 million, for the constitution drafted by the MRP and the Socialists. Eight million voters abstained, reflecting both lack of interest and ambivalence about de Gaulle in particular. On that less than overwhelming note, the Fourth Republic at last became a reality as France gingerly stepped out of the Liberation era and into the postwar world.

FRANCE BETWEEN THE SUPERPOWERS

The Second World War completed two global processes begun by the First World War: the dismantling of Europe's world hegemony and the rise of the United States and the Soviet Union to superpower status. Whereas during the late nineteenth century London and Paris dominated international diplomacy, in the years from 1945 to 1990 Washington and Moscow would assume pride of place. One of the most pressing issues confronting the French in the years after the Liberation was adjusting to a bipolar world, one in which France would no longer be one of the great powers but rather subject to the whims and agendas of stronger nations. More specifically, would France have to choose between the American or Soviet camps, or could it retain an independent perspective? Ultimately the Cold War forced the French, like most other peoples in Europe, to take sides, firmly joining the Western powers. Yet this was a choice made by the French for their own reasons, not simply imposed by Washington. Moreover, France retained a degree of distance between its policies and those of the United States that would prove a frequent source of irritation to American policy-makers in the years to come.

Although by far the most likely scenario, France's membership in the American camp during the Cold War was by no means automatic nor predetermined. The Soviet Union enjoyed great prestige in France at the end of the war, and the model of Soviet Communism appealed to many. In spite of the liberation of western Europe by British and North American troops, the Soviet Union deserved the lion's share of the credit for crushing Hitler's *Wehrmacht*: the Red Flag, not the Stars and Stripes, flew over conquered Berlin. In the years after 1944 municipalities throughout France, especially but not only in the Communist-dominated working-class suburbs of Paris, renamed streets *rue Stalinegrad* in honour of Russia's great military victory. This military prestige won the Soviets sympathy from many French patriots with little love for socialism, as did the general left-wing atmosphere of the French Resistance. The French intelligentsia in particular often praised the USSR uncritically in the years after the Liberation. Then there was the massive presence of the French Communist Party, the choice of one out of every four French voters, not to mention the fact that the Red Army remained the largest and most powerful military force in Europe.

Nonetheless, a Soviet France was never a realistic prospect in postwar Europe, and not simply because the Red Army never set foot on French soil. More significantly, neither the French people nor Stalin himself desired a Communist regime in Paris. Although the PCF could count on a large share of the French electorate in the immediate postwar years, it never came close to a majority. Moreover, those who did vote Communist did so for a variety of reasons, not necessarily because they hoped for a Marxist transformation of society. At the same time, the Soviet Union had no desire to pursue a new French revolution. As Stalin made clear to the Western Allies at the end of the war, he foresaw a postwar Europe divided between East and West, with the former controlled by Moscow and the latter under the authority of the United States. He felt granting Washington a free hand in the West would in exchange secure him American consent to his dominance of Eastern Europe. He also hoped such a strategic compromise would encourage the United States to continue its wartime aid to the Soviets, aid seen as vital to rebuilding his shattered nation. In addition, Stalin believed an independent France would be far more useful as a counterweight to American and British policies than would a Communist-dominated one, and looked to the re-establishment of France as a great power in postwar Europe. In line with this perspective, the PCF dropped all mention of revolution after the Liberation, preaching instead the necessity of rebuilding the nation's economy and restoring France to greatness.

If Stalin wished to use France to restrain the Americans, many French and de Gaulle in particular had similar ideas about cultivating the Soviets to balance the influence of the United States. Since the late nineteenth century the idea of a diplomatic and military alliance with Russia had strongly appealed to many French leaders, giving rise to both the Triple Entente of 1907 and the 1935 mutual assistance pact. Keeping Germany on the defensive was the main goal of such agreements, and in part this remained true after 1945. Both France and the Soviet Union had suffered invasion and devastation from Nazi Germany, and both looked askance at American plans to restore that nation, in particular rearming her. Yet in the new era a Franco-Soviet alliance could also enable both nations to resist pressures from the United States. While Charles de Gaulle made no secret of his dislike of Communism and did his best to contain the power of the PCF in the Resistance, he very much favoured strategic accords with the USSR. This view led him to Moscow in November 1944 on a goodwill visit. The next month France and the Soviet Union signed an alliance, one that had few practical consequences but served to notify the Americans that France did indeed have diplomatic options.

All such manifestations of independence aside, the basic reality was that France did become an American ally, to a certain extent even an American satellite, in the years after the Second World War. Although the two nations developed a complex relationship, it arose in the context of the unquestioned economic and military superiority of the United States. Whereas America emerged from the war by far the wealthiest nation in the world, France was desperately poor and in need of massive assistance to rebuild its economy, assistance that could only come from Washington. Its straitened material circumstances forced France, always a proud nation, to go begging cap in hand to the Americans for help in restoring itself. The United States certainly wanted to take part in the reconstruction of France, but it had its own ideas about the shape of postwar Europe. American policy-makers envisioned a Europe that would be peaceful, united, and a rich market and site of investment for American capital. In deciding how to aid France, these American ideas generally took precedence over French desires.

Wartime Franco-American relations had never been trouble-free, and these tensions continued into the postwar era. The enmity between de Gaulle and Franklin Delano Roosevelt had been notorious, so much so that Roosevelt wished to see France ruled by an American military government, not a Gaullist provisional one, immediately after the Liberation. While French civilians initially greeted American soldiers as liberators, by 1945 many began to complain about the arrogance of the typical GI, and to suggest that France had exchanged a German occupation for an American one. Among some intellectuals the prewar stereotype of American culture as artificial, mediocre, and soulless received a new lease on life. The notorious 1947 'Coca-colonization' feud, in which the PCF and the powerful French wine industry joined forces to block the marketing of America's classic beverage in France, provided an example of this tension. Such knee-jerk anti-Americanism, frequently commented upon in the American press, was stereotypical rather than universal; many French still looked upon the United States fondly. Nonetheless, cultural differences and tensions also played a role in the development of the relationship between the two countries.

Early in 1946 Léon Blum, head of the Socialist Party, led a major French delegation to Washington with the aim of securing American financial aid. The French requested a loan of $3 billion which would enable them to import both food for their people and industrial raw materials to restart the national economy. In considering the French request, the Americans had several goals in mind. Economically, they wished France to bring inflation under control and make a clear commitment to free trade, in effect the unimpeded access of American goods to French markets. Politically, they wanted to hold the line against Soviet power, both in France and in Europe, and to win French support for the rebuilding of Germany as a bulwark against that power. The resulting Blum–Byrnes accord of May 1946 satisfied neither party. France only got a loan of $650 million, not enough to make a significant difference in its fortunes. Moreover, France made major concessions to the American film industry, concessions that would ensure Hollywood's dominance of French movie theatres for years to come. At the same time, France remained sceptical of a revived Germany, and committed to a major role for the Left in French politics.

The Blum–Byrnes accord underscored the interrelationship of domestic politics and foreign policy in France's relationship to the United States. This was made even clearer by the Marshall Plan, America's financial aid pro-gramme for rebuilding Europe. In June 1947, American Secretary of State George Marshall announced a new, more systematic initiative to channel American resources to Europe. The Marshall Plan replaced loans with large monetary grants, but these grants did not come without strings attached. Not only did it stipulate that monies be used to buy American products, thus reaffirming the American ideal of free trade, but also gave American policy experts the right to intervene directly in French economic and financial structures. US officials thus encouraged the French to develop a more rational tax structure and take firmer measures against inflation. Moreover, French acceptance of Marshall Plan aid spelled the defeat of its resistance to Washington's plans for a revived, Western-oriented Germany. By the end of 1947 Paris had given up its plans for an autonomous Rhine-land, and accepted the integration of the French occupied zone into what would soon become West Germany.

The knottiest problem of all was the left-wing nature of domestic French politics, especially the powerful presence of the PCF. By 1947 the Cold War made any cooperation between the United States and the Soviet Union, or their respective allies, impossible. American policy-makers found it increasingly difficult to accept aiding a nation with representatives of the enemy camp in its government. Ultimately, the desire of many French women and men to preserve the unity of the Resistance failed, and France took sides in the Cold War. However, developments within French politics contributed to this outcome as much, if not more, than pressure from foreign capitals.

FROM TRIPARTISM TO THE THIRD FORCE

From January 1946 to May 1947 France was governed by a coalition of the three largest political parties – the Socialists, Communists and MRP – in a system known as Tripartism. Unlike many coalition governments, Tri-partism was more than a political marriage of convenience. It constituted the last gasp of the anti-fascist tradition in France, the heir to the Popular Front of the 1930s and the wartime Resistance. Moreover, as in Italy (where a Tripartite government also ruled briefly after the war), Tripartism rejected the bipolar politics of the Cold War in favour of a broad-based movement of progressive reform. It symbolised the hope that the wartime spirit of Resistance unity could survive the division of the world into American and Soviet blocs. The brief lifespan of Tripartism thus marked the final break between the war and the postwar era, underlying France's inability to resist entanglement in the conflict between the USSR and the USA.

The first Tripartite administration formed after the departure of de Gaulle, with the colourless Socialist Felix Gouin as prime minister. The leaders of the three parties also drew up a vague Tripartite Charter, which called for a variety of progressive reforms. Given that the Tripartite parties devoted most of 1946 to figuring out a permanent system of government for France, however, Tripartism as a systematic ruling structure only assumed concrete shape at the beginning of 1947, when Vincent Auriol of the Socialists was elected the first president of the Fourth Republic. His fellow Socialist Paul Ramadier became prime minister, succeeding the five-week caretaker government of Léon Blum. Certain rules governed the Tripartite coalition. Above all, its leaders needed demonstrable ties to the Resistance. For example, although Paul Ramadier had not taken part in the underground anti-fascist struggle, he had voted against awarding full powers to Marshal Pétain in 1940. The coalition also had to include ministers from all three participating parties. Of particular concern was the PCF request for the Ministries of Foreign Affairs, the Interior, and Defence, since Communist control of similar positions in Eastern European coalitions had led directly to Sovietization. The Communists did receive four ministerial portfolios in the Ramadier government, including Defence, yet the latter was structured to ensure that real power remained with the prime minister. Finally, no one party could be allowed to grow too powerful, thus threatening the stability of the coalition. The Socialists were allowed to select the prime minister not only because of their ideological position between the PCF and MRP, but also because they were the weakest of the three parties. By the beginning of 1947 many viewed the PCF as the greatest danger to the system, a view that international events would soon reinforce.

The first major blow to Tripartite unity came from the empire. In November 1946 negotiations between the French and the Vietminh, Vietnam's Communist resistance movement, broke down when the French Navy shelled Haiphong harbour in the course of trying to establish French control over its prewar colony. French troops followed up this assault with a full-scale invasion of northern Vietnam, prompting massive armed resistance by the Vietminh. The short-lived Blum government proved unable to contain the mounting crisis, so that by January 1947 the Vietminh officially declared independence. This placed the French Communists in an extremely awkward position. They had supported the Vietminh, and colonial liberation movements in general, a stance which now ran directly counter to the policy of their own governing coalition. Moreover, the intensification of armed conflicts between Communists and non-Communists in Greece and China led many in France to conclude that the Indochina war was merely part of a global struggle between rival political systems, one in which the PCF stood opposed to the interests of the nation.

This belief soon found reinforcement in the attitude of the Americans towards French Tripartism. In March 1947, President Truman unveiled the famous Truman Doctrine, pledging the United States to resist Communist expansion everywhere in the world. For France, the Truman Doctrine implied that Washington was less likely than ever to tolerate Tripartism, but that in contrast increased American aid might follow the ousting of the PCF from the government. The winter of 1946/47 was a very harsh one, necessitating further reductions in the official bread ration. Given this context, the prospect of trans-Atlantic dollars seemed ever more alluring. For the MRP and increasingly important sections of the Socialist Party, therefore, both foreign and domestic considerations combined to render the alliance with the PCF less and less tolerable.

The PCF was itself also affected by the poor condition of the economy, and its impact upon the party's working-class constituents. Ever since the Liberation, France's Communists had preached the 'Battle of Production', emphasising the need to restore the national economy rather than fighting for wage increases and other specifically working-class interests. However, the unchecked inflationary spiral of the postwar years, combined with the PCF and union policy of wage restraint, meant declining real wages for most French labourers. These difficult conditions were made all the more galling by the flamboyant opulence of the *nouveaux riche*, whose luxury not only contrasted bitterly with the privations of working people, but also made a mockery of the egalitarian ethos upon which the very idea of the Battle of Production rested. By the early months of 1947 French workers were less and less willing to sacrifice their living standards for the good of the nation. The PCF found itself caught between the continued insistence of its coalition partners on fighting inflation through low wages, and the ever-increasing complaints of its own constituents.

Something had to give. Ramadier's government adopted a classic policy of deflation in order to deal with the economic crisis, and the PCF loyally supported it. Many French workers had had enough, however. On 30 April 20,000 workers at the (now nationalised) Renault auto plant went on strike in a clear protest against low wages and inflation. The strike forced the PCF to choose; after complicated manoeuvres between the Socialists, the MRP and the PCF, the four government ministers of the latter party voted no confidence in Ramadier's administration. They refused to resign, and

Ramadier fired them on 5 May, ending PCF membership in his coalition government, and bringing Tripartism to an end. Now freed from ties to the administration the PCF moved sharply to an oppositionist stance, championing the grievances of French workers and demanding pay increases for them. Both this new political situation and the ever-declining economy produced an upsurge in popular militancy during the rest of 1947. Dockworkers, railway workers and others went on strike, and a series of food riots spread throughout the country. On the Right, Gaullist forces mounted an offensive against the weakened Ramadier government, creating a new political party, the Rally of the French People (RPF). Not since the Liberation had France experienced such political turmoil.

The crisis reached a head in November when Ramadier decided to abolish the coal subsidy and raise utility and transport rates in order to protect the stability of the franc. This immediately triggered a massive strike wave in Paris and throughout the country, the number of strikers reaching three million by the beginning of December. Led by the General Confederation of Labour (CGT), the strike turned violent in many areas, assuming the character of a near-insurrection in Marseilles. The government responded by passing a harsh anti-strike bill and sending troops to fight the strikers in coal mining areas. Above all, it appealed to moderate public opinion by portraying the strike as less a dispute over wages than a Communist attempt to seize power. These measures proved successful in breaking the strike by the middle of December. Non-Communist forces in the CGT split off to form their own union organisation (covertly aided by American funds), thus further reducing the strength of organised labour in France. The final defeat came a year later with the failure of a seven-week national coal strike in November 1948, one characterised by the jailing and dismissal of thousands of miners and a police occupation of the coal fields.

The ousting of the PCF and the collapse of Tripartism brought to a definitive end not just the attempt to preserve the unity of the Resistance, but the entire tradition of political anti-fascism that had begun with the Popular Front. France now chose sides in the Cold War, a choice dictated as much by domestic considerations as by foreign pressures. Henceforth the governments of the Fourth Republic would be governed by centrist coalitions of the Socialists, the MRP and the Radicals. The Communists and Gaullists were both consigned to the margins of a system that increasingly resembled that of the Third Republic. By the end of 1948 the basic outlines of what came to be called the 'Third Force' were already in place. As France moved into the 1950s, the heady days of the victory over fascism, and the rosy hopes for social justice and political renewal, seemed a very long way away.

The failure of Tripartism and the stabilisation of the Fourth Republic demonstrated two basic facts about postwar French life. First, France did take its place in the new Cold War, choosing the American over the Soviet bloc. Secondly, in the establishment of the Fourth Republic the French rejected the new departures represented by both de Gaulle and the PCF, opting instead for the familiarity of weak parliamentary structures similar to those they had known before 1940. However, this is not to argue that France became an American puppet, nor that it simply retreated into the past. The nation retained considerable independence in its dealings with the Americans, and its international position arose much more from domestic considerations than Washington's desires. France retained significant ties with the Soviet Union, for example, and its attitudes towards both Britain and the new West Germany differed markedly from those of the United States.

Neither did the adoption of a somewhat antiquated parliamentary system represent unwillingness to embrace the future. On the contrary, the years of the Fourth Republic brought about some of the most dramatic social and cultural changes France experienced during the twentieth century, so that the nation of 1960 was in many respects unrecognisable from the vantage point of twenty years earlier. This birth of a new France, and the ways in which the political structures of the Fourth Republic facilitated it, will form the subject of the next chapter.

CHAPTER THREE

THE *TRENTE GLORIEUSES*

Few French regimes have achieved a more paradoxical record than the Fourth Republic. A failure in some important respects, at the same time the regime that governed France from 1946 to 1958 scored major achievements in others. Politically, the Republic disappointed those in France who hoped to translate the spirit of the Resistance into a more efficient, equitable, and morally pure system of government. Instead, the Fourth Republic seemed to replicate all the inadequacies of the Third, with its unstable governments and ineffective politicians. Likewise, the postwar regime failed to overcome the serious class divisions in French society, so that a powerful Communist Party remained as a symbol of industrial conflict and working-class alienation. In addition, as will be discussed in the following chapter, French dreams of using the empire to restore France to great power status after 1945 had largely come to naught by the end of the Republic in 1958. During its brief twelve-year existence, therefore, the French Fourth Republic in some respects represented the disenchantment many in France felt with the fruits of victory.

Yet when we consider the economic and social legacy of this regime, an entirely different portrait emerges. Under the Fourth Republic France began the unprecedented period of economic expansion and prosperity known as the *trente glorieuses*, or thirty glorious years. This era of growth and good times fundamentally reshaped the nation, infusing it with a sense of optimism and dynamism without parallel during the previous century. France urbanised, became more middle class, developed impressive new technologies, and in many other ways transformed the life of its ordinary citizens. The old France of charming villages, traditional families and luxury consumer goods like fine wines and silk stockings did not entirely disappear, but nonetheless gave way to a new France of superhighways, skyscrapers and computers. Whereas some bemoaned the loss of a distinctive national character and the uncritical rush towards consumerism, others welcomed the new opportunities that peace and prosperity afforded.

The economic expansion of the third quarter of the twentieth century was not of course limited to France alone, but characterised the Western world in general during the postwar era of American global dominance. However, policies and events specific to France shaped the postwar boom. Both the Fourth Republic and its successor, the Fifth Republic, adopted policies that broke with long-standing French traditions and set forth new patterns. At the same time popular attitudes changed, as more people began to think in terms of future opportunities rather than past difficulties. The two phenomena worked together to create a vibrant new vision of an ancient nation. For many French people the war and Occupation had finally killed off the long nineteenth century represented by the Third Republic, without however determining what would replace it. The economic boom that started in the late 1940s provided a definitive model of the nation's future. Under its impetus, in the thirty years after the Second World War France leaped headlong into modernity.

PLANNING FOR PROSPERITY

Under the Third Republic France had been widely known as a country of both undoubted wealth and also economic stagnation. While fortunate in possessing rich agricultural lands and industrial raw materials as well as a highly educated and skilled population, the nation's business leaders seemed to lack the dynamism and vision of their counterparts in Britain, Germany or America. Many believed that rampant class conflict undermined the ability of the French to work together for the betterment of all. The Depression of the 1930s confirmed this bleak prospect of a nation unable to translate its numerous resources into a prosperous future for all its citizens. For the Left, prosperity and better living standards represented challenges that were political as well as economic. Activists in the Popular Front and the Resistance had condemned fascism not just as an authoritarian political system, but also one that created and perpetuated poverty and class inequalities. Accordingly, a key aspect of the anti-fascist agenda had been the creation of decent living standards for all of the people of France. For many this meant some form of socialism, for others a reformed and more productive capitalism. But the need for prosperity was something upon which all parties of the Resistance, from Gaullists to Communists, could agree.

This unity of purpose provides one explanation for the impressive growth of the French economy in the thirty years following the end of the Second World War. Never in its history had France known such economic dynamism. In general, the nation's economy grew at the very healthy rate of 5 per cent per year, achieving rates of up to 10 per cent per year during the late 1950s and early 1960s. French industry prospered, especially heavy industry, dispelling forever the idea of the nation as a land of artisans and handicrafts. For example, the number of cars made in France grew from 750,000 in 1951 to four million in 1958, and the number of tractors grew by a factor of ten from 1946 to 1958. Within ten years after the Liberation, the slogan 'Produce!' had gone from a clarion call of the anti-fascist Left to a solid reality (Rioux, 1987).

Political will alone did not explain this massive expansion, of course. The postwar era was a time of great prosperity throughout the Western world. One key factor in the revival of the French economy was the American Marshall Plan. Under this programme the United States contributed over $15 billion to France in the shape of credits, loans and grants. Whereas the first French governments spent some of this money on food, the majority was invested in industrial reconstruction. The birth of European economic integration also played a key role. In 1950 Foreign Minister Robert Schuman proposed creating an organisation to coordinate coal and steel production between France and West Germany. From an Alsatian family, Schuman was especially sensitive to the Franco-German rivalries that had torn Europe apart twice in the century, and felt that industrial cooperation could both prevent such political conflict and benefit the economies of both nations. In 1951 he helped create the European Coal and Steel Community, including France, West Germany, Italy, Belgium, the Netherlands and Luxembourg, to regulate price and production levels among the member nations. This organisation gave way in 1957 to the European Economic Community (EEC), or Common Market. The creation of a large, tariff-free economic zone provided a major stimulus to French exports, both agricultural and industrial.

Yet French domestic policies also bear much of the credit for the economic boom. In seeking to restore and ultimately revolutionise the French economy after the war, the French turned to a technique usually associated with authoritarian governments – centralised economic planning. In January 1946, the government set up the new Commisariat Générale du Plan, under the directorship of brandy merchant Jean Monnet. Monnet had been the only prominent French businessman to join de Gaulle in his London exile, and during the war had represented French business interests in Washington. While much of the political inspiration for what became known as *planisme* came from the anti-fascist Resistance, the idea also owed a certain debt to Vichy's tradition of state planning. Indeed, the initial blueprints for the Planning Office were largely copied from the planning agency established by Vichy in 1941. Finally, the Jacobin tradition of the centralised state as the initiator of progressive political change, so dear to the French Left ever since the great Revolution, also gave state economic planning a clear mandate in the hungry years after the Liberation.

Jean Monnet rejected both the authoritarian state planning of Vichy, and the heavy emphasis on state economic ownership of the socialist model.

Instead, he saw the job of the Planning Commissariat as making capitalism operate more rationally and efficiently, by coordinating the actions of industry, labour, and the state sector, and by channelling scarce resources where they would do the most good. In particular, Monnet was able to use the nationalised banking sector to direct the flow of industrial capital. The Commissariat was a small body of about forty which answered only to the prime minister, and thus was able to plan the recovery without parliamentary oversight. Members of the plan organised a variety of committees, including representatives of labour, business and the public sector, to plan the new French economy. The business community accepted planning as a much better alternative than nationalisation, and labour and the Left enthusiastically embraced it as a socialistic type of economic rationalisation.

The first priority was, of course, postwar recovery. The Commissariat immediately set a goal for the nation's economy of returning to 1938 (i.e., prewar) production levels by the end of 1946, and in fact achieved this goal by early 1947. That same year the Commissariat initiated its first Five Year Plan. This plan took as its primary goal industrial development, and more generally breaking away from the stagnation so characteristic of the economy under the Third Republic. It identified a few basic industrial sectors as key, including coal, electricity and transport, and for each industry established guidelines and production targets. Private companies who cooperated with the Plan received priority in the allocation of key raw materials. Monnet was able to overcome the primary obstacle to the Plan, a lack of adequate investment capital, by using Marshall Plan funds. In addition, the Plan sought to address some long-term weaknesses of the French economy by creating new information and managerial resources. It created the National Institute of Statistical Studies (INSEE) to improve knowledge about the economy, reorganised and improved the National Council for Scientific Research (CNRS) and, perhaps most important, founded the National Administration School (ENA) to train the nation's leading civil servants. ENA graduates would play such an important role in French administration that some began to refer to France as an 'Enarchy'. In Monnet's view, mobilising the intellectual resources of the nation was key to building prosperity for the new generation.

By the end of the first Five Year Plan in 1952 Monnet could look back upon some solid successes. True, the Plan had not achieved its stated goal of boosting French production levels 25 per cent above those of 1929 (or pre-Depression levels). Also, the departure of the CGT and the Communists from planning organisations after 1947 had dealt a serious blow to his dreams of cooperation between private industry and labour. Nonetheless, by 1952 the Plan had raised France's gross national product 39 per cent over 1946, and the economy had achieved a very respectable growth rate of

4.5 per cent per year. More specifically, the Plan rebuilt the nation's transportation sector, so badly damaged by the war, and made solid progress in boosting coal production and electrical output, especially through heavy investment in hydroelectric power. Most significantly, it had proved that France could modernise its economy, laying down a blueprint for further progress.

Part of the nature of Monnet's planning process was a system of priorities; he recognised that all needs could not be addressed at the same time. Accordingly, in privileging industrial recovery and growth the first Five Year Plan neglected other economic problems, notably housing, agriculture and consumer goods. While production had increased sharply, the purchasing power of French consumers had stagnated. Translating economic growth into prosperity for the average French woman and man was the primary goal of the second Plan, 1952–57. The new Plan set itself several economic goals, such as raising the gross national product by 25 per cent, and exceeded all of them. The government worked to modernise French agriculture, promoting the use of farm machinery and chemical fertilisers, favouring larger, more efficient farms, and encouraging farmers to move from more heavily populated regions to less densely settled ones. Housing was a particularly grave problem. France had long had some of the worst housing stock in Western Europe; as late as 1950 85 per cent of the housing units in Paris pre-dated the *First* World War. The second Plan placed special emphasis on new housing construction, building over 1 million new housing units. A significant percentage of these were built in massive, high-rise public housing blocks, known as *habitations à loyer modéré* (HLM). These new buildings sprouted like weeds throughout the suburbs of Paris and other French cities, radically transforming the social and visual landscape of France's urban life.

By the end of the Fourth Republic centralised economic planning had demonstrated beyond the shadow of a doubt its ability to revive and renew the nation's economy. After 1957 the French government would implement four more economic plans, the last one concluding in 1970. While benefiting from a very favourable economic conjuncture, in planning its new economy France proved that it could change the practices of a century and achieve prosperity on its own terms, employing practices that were uniquely French.

THE CONSUMER REVOLUTION OF THE 1960s

If the Fourth Republic sowed the seeds of postwar prosperity, the Fifth Republic reaped the harvest. During the golden years from 1958 to 1970 the French economy grew at a spectacular rate, averaging 5.8 per cent per year. During this period France enjoyed the most dynamic economy in

Europe; in all the world, only Japan could boast healthier growth rates. As under the Fourth Republic, during the 1960s the French state played a major role in directing economic expansion. The planning process continued, with the government coordinating the programmes of private sector business through its control of finances, statistical information and industrial raw materials. It promoted a process of corporate modernisation, spurring a wave of business mergers to create larger, more efficient firms. Most important, the French government abandoned the nation's traditional protectionism and worked hard to build a business sector capable of competing in international markets. Exports grew from less than 10 per cent of French production in 1958 to 17 per cent in 1970, and other European countries, especially West Germany, replaced France's colonies as its most important trading partners. This new internationalism, where France exported not just silk stockings and fine wines but cars, aeroplanes and other industrial products, symbolised the new dynamic France of the postwar years.

Much more so than during the Fourth Republic, this economic growth translated into visible increases in prosperity and changes in lifestyle during the 1960s. At the root of both lay a change that had begun quietly during the grim years of the Occupation, yet had momentous consequences for postwar France. For nearly a century, from the 1850s to the 1940s, France had been notorious for having among the lowest birth rates in Europe. A major cause of national concern by the beginning of the twentieth century, the problem of low natality had only been increased by the bloodletting of the First World War. By the interwar years the nation had gone past zero population growth to a steady excess of deaths over births. Fears of population loss shaped all areas of national life, from the promotion of immigration and imperial expansion as ways to compensate, to efforts to boost the birth rate by banning abortion and restricting birth control. The Vichy state granted subsidies to large families, prosecuted abortionists as murderers, and in general regarded low birth rates as a moral failing and a central reason for the defeat of 1940.

For reasons that are hard to explain, France's birth rate finally began to increase during the Occupation. Increased natality usually reflects economic prosperity and a general spirit of optimism in the future, phenomena notably absent during the war years. It seems that the pro-natalist policies of Vichy, building upon those of the Third Republic, finally began to bear fruit. Changes in popular attitudes, such as the increasing popularity of marriage and having more than two children, also played a role. The result was a sharp jump in the number of births, from 600,000 per year in the late 1930s to over 800,000 per year in the late 1940s and 1950s. France's population grew from 40 million on the eve of the Second World War to over 50 million by 1970. A notable decline in mortality rates also contributed to the population growth, as did large-scale immigration from elsewhere in Europe.

But statistics only begin to tell the story. France's new fecundity had a dramatic, massive impact upon French society, so much so that, according to humourists, the classic Revolutionary phrase of 'Liberty, Equality, Fraternity' had been replaced by 'Liberty, Equality, Maternity'. The flood of new babies had an immediate effect on large sectors of national life. Specifically, the French had to enlarge and modernise their often archaic hospital and health care infrastructure in response to the demands of increased maternity. Soon French day care centres and schools began feeling the impacts of the baby boom. The number of French secondary school students nearly doubled in the ten years between 1948 and 1958. The push for improvements in housing was largely fuelled by a concern for the well-being of France's new large families, so that ideas of domesticity and happy home life became a major postwar preoccupation. Finally, the jump in natality provided a significant stimulus to many industries. The new French fascination with and adoration of the new generation prompted a threefold increase in the purchase of toys in the postwar years. They also stimulated the dairy industry, and were a key cause for investment in durable consumer products, especially those oriented towards the home, like refrigerators and washing and drying machines.

The postwar baby boom was consequently the single most important factor in launching France's new consumer society. After all, babies, and the families who bore them, seemed to need so many *things*! More generally, the presence of so many young people both reflected and created a sense of optimism, of dynamism and faith in the future that at times translated into a desire to spend rather than save, to enjoy life today confident in the belief that tomorrow would be even better. Changes in state policy also helped promote the new consumerism. The Fourth Republic's creation of an extensive social welfare system, including Social Security coverage, subsidised medical care, pensions for the elderly, and a minimum wage, encouraged people to spend more in at least two different ways. Not only did it grant French people a level of security not dependent upon their individual savings, but also, by creating thousands of secure state jobs in the new social welfare bureaucracy, provided a new level of guaranteed employment. In any case, the prosperity and low unemployment levels of the 1950s and 1960s meant that people could buy more freely, especially big-ticket items on credit, without worrying about losing their jobs and their ability to pay for them. By the end of the 1950s, therefore, it seemed that the stable affluence and prosperity so long dreamed of had finally arrived, and it was now time for the French to enjoy the good life.

What did the French buy? Large home appliances, especially refrigerators and washing machines, were very popular, with three-quarters of

French households owning them by 1975. One of the most dramatic symbols of the new consumerism was the television, unknown before the war, which became a standard part of the furnishing of French living rooms in the 1960s. In fact, a measure of the changes it brought to France was the fact that, in the classic land of gastronomy, it now became common for families to eat dinner while watching TV! New modes of transportation, above all the private automobile, also accounted for much consumer spending. By the end of the 1960s the vast majority of French families owned their own cars. The desire for travel also fed the burgeoning tourist industry, as did the government's establishment of three weeks paid vacation in 1956 (extended to four weeks in 1963). In 1967, 21 million French people went on vacation, including 3 million who went abroad. Finally, a fundamental shift in French spending patterns deserves mention here. In the nineteenth and early twentieth centuries the French were often noted for spending a greater percentage of their incomes on food, and a lower percentage on housing, than most other Europeans. This changed during the postwar era: whereas in 1959 the French spent 38 per cent and 16 per cent of their incomes on food and housing, respectively, these proportions had shifted to 25 per cent and 20 per cent by 1975. In short, the people of France were spending less on food (although, thanks to increased agricultural efficiency, both quantity and quality of consumption grew), more on housing and other expensive, durable consumer goods (Berstein, 1993).

The new consumerism generated its own series of anxieties. Some social commentators feared that, as in the biblical tale of Jacob and Esau, the French were selling their souls for a mess of potage. Georges Perec's 1965 novel *Les Choses* (*Things*) trenchantly criticised the new spirit of materialism, and in his science fiction classic *Alphaville*, made the same year, filmmaker Jean-Luc Godard referred to HLMs as 'hospitals for long-term maladies', implying that they brainwashed their inhabitants. Some hoped, or feared, that the wave of buying would wipe out class distinctions and spell the end of the political Left. However, before writing off the postwar consumer revolution as an outburst of shallow hedonism one should consider at least two factors. First, the new prosperity did relatively little to erase strong class distinctions in French society, or to make the nation more egalitarian. French workers might enjoy better housing and home appliances by the 1960s, but they (and usually their children as well) remained working class, shut off from many of the perks of bourgeois society. In 1970, for example, 5 per cent of the population owned 45 per cent of the national wealth, and 10 per cent lived below the poverty line. If anything, the long period of prosperity increased social and economic inequalities, as often happens in dynamic capitalist systems.

Secondly, one must remember that the dream of prosperity was not simply a capitalist fantasy, but a hope very much rooted in the spirit of the Resistance. There is no necessary contradiction between enjoying the good life and remaining loyal to the Left; one can be a Communist and still go on vacation. The example of vacations is very much to the point here. Often taken as a symbol of wasteful luxury, the new postwar emphasis on time off and travel arose directly out of the Popular Front's tradition of mass organised leisure as a political goal. Even the much-maligned Club Méditerrané, the famous organised vacation company founded in 1950, was shaped and led by Gilbert Trigano, a Jewish veteran of the Communist Resistance. Club Med's programmes, such as the use of beads instead of money at its resorts, revealed not only marketing savvy but a considerable amount of social engineering and egalitarianism as well. Therefore, in considering the postwar consumer explosion that did so much to transform modern France, one must regard it as one of the most significant fruits of the anti-fascist struggle. It may not have created Heaven on earth, but in at least ameliorating the pangs of poverty and giving millions access to a new standard of living it went a long way towards making the sacrifices of the Resistance worthwhile.

THE CHANGING FACE OF FRENCH SOCIETY

In postwar France, economic growth interacted with social change. By the end of the *trente glorieuses* in the mid-1970s not only had the nation's population grown significantly, but also the conditions of different social groups within it had shifted to an important degree. Like the economy, French society in the thirty years after the Liberation demonstrated a new dynamism that contrasted sharply with the stagnation of the interwar years. Three groups in particular, women, youth and immigrants, assumed a new significance in French society, and their collective experiences provide a revealing glimpse into the new make-up of modern France after 1945.

In spite of the tendency to view the French as champions of the feminine, during its modern history France has been a decidedly patriarchal society, one in which the *coq Gaulois* generally reigned supreme. The fact that the postwar era began with the granting of female suffrage, a generation later than most other Western nations, indicated a new day in France, but also showed how far the nation had to travel towards full gender equality. During the war French women had worked in the Resistance alongside men, and more generally laboured at many masculine tasks in place of fathers, husbands, brothers and sons absent as prisoners of war. Granting them the vote was seen as a recognition of their labour for France, as well as part of the progressive agenda of the new Republic.

Yet, as in many other areas, the hopes of the Resistance for full gender equality did not last long into the postwar era. Although women could now not only vote but run for office, the number of female members of the National Assembly not only remained small but actually declined from the late 1940s to the 1960s. Women constituted 7 per cent of parliamentary deputies in 1946, but only 2 per cent in 1968. This lack of political influence reflected a continued inegality in society and culture as a whole. As elsewhere in Western Europe and America, the end of the war witnessed a renewed emphasis on family life, all the more striking in France due to the nation's long history of low fertility. Both women and men embraced the ideal of the woman as mother, whose primary duty was to create a comfortable, loving home life for her husband and children. The massive growth of the home appliances industry underlined this view of women as housewives, helping to build the new France by keeping their kitchens and bathrooms clean and hygienic. At the same time the fashion industry reasserted the beauty of the feminine. Christian Dior's New Look of 1947 emphasised feminine proportions, and the idea that a woman's beauty lay in being as different from a man as possible.

In such a climate of traditional family values, arguments for women's equality made little popular headway. In 1949 Simone de Beauvoir published her landmark work *The Second Sex*, arguing that equality before the law would not by itself empower women, but that they needed economic and political strength as well. Yet relatively few French women listened to de Beauvoir's message. In a society where living conditions for women and families at last seemed to be improving substantially, issues of gender inequality lacked immediacy. In contrast, women's magazines like *Marie-France*, *Marie-Claire* and especially *Elle* proved enormously popular in the postwar years. Their emphasis on beauty, cooking, home appliances and romance (but not politics or careers) repackaged classic ideas about the woman's sphere as modern and attractive.

The continued inequality of women in postwar France in part arose from (and also helped perpetuate) legal and institutional disadvantages. Until 1964, for example, a married woman needed her husband's permission to open a bank account. Unequal treatment before the law in matters of property and divorce persisted until the late 1970s. The upper reaches of government administration, business and academia remained largely male preserves; only in 1980, for example, did the prestigious French Academy admit its first woman member. At the same time, popular attitudes preserved the social divide between men and women. Many French people, of both sexes, believed sexual equality meant sexual sameness, and instead upheld the idea of difference as both natural and desirable. Many regarded feminism as primarily an Anglo-Saxon idea, taken from nations that put less importance upon femininity than did France. Women should be treated well, both French men and women seemed to argue, but above all they should be treated like women. Not until the student uprisings of May 1968 did postwar France witness the birth of a significant feminist movement, and even then French feminism lagged behind its counterparts elsewhere in terms of power and influence.

Yet one would be very much mistaken in viewing postwar French women as quiescent or stuck in the past. Women bought household appliances because they believed they would make their lives easier and more fulfilling, not because they wanted to restore the world of their mothers. Moreover, the new prosperity of the 1950s and 1960s underlay changes in social and sexual mores that became more evident after 1968. By the mid-1960s, for example, premarital sex for girls was becoming more common, if not yet the norm. In 1967 the French government finally repealed the archaic 1920 law banning contraception. The 1970s would bring further changes, such as the appearance of small but militant feminist movements and the legalisation of abortion rights. Although France still had a long way to travel down the road towards gender equality, the dynamism of the postwar era offered new possibilities to French women, giving ideas of female equality a new significance.

The impact of the postwar boom on France's young people was much more immediate and dramatic. Thanks to the upsurge in the birth rate, the nation soon counted far more children than it had for a long time, and the tidal wave of babies not only spurred the consumer revolution but helped reshape French society in general. The number of people under the age of twenty-five in France doubled during the twenty years after the war, far outstripping the general rate of population growth. Children and young people now represented the dynamism of postwar France, its youthful character, just as during the interwar years the aging of the population had symbolised a stagnant nation in decline. By the mid-1960s this new generation had become old enough to speak for itself, and what it had to say did not always please its elders. As elsewhere in Europe and America, the postwar era witnessed the rise of mass-based youth cultures, young people who identified neither as children nor adults, but something in between. Consequently, French youth represented the rejuvenation of the nation, and a new, sometimes troubling element in an ancient society.

The nation's educational system felt the effects of the baby boom most directly. Not only did the 800,000 babies born every year after 1946 on average create a massive new demand for schooling, but the new emphasis on children often translated into a much greater desire for education as the key to future success. Demography alone created a need for more teachers, classrooms and educational materials, but the changing social role of education imposed its own demands and problems. The pressures of growth were felt most acutely at the level of the secondary schools, and then the universities. Before 1945 secondary education in France was largely the preserve of society's elites. Whereas after the age of fourteen rural and working-class youth generally left school to go to work, children of the well-to-do would attend the nation's *lycées*, famed for their emphasis on rigorous classical education and brilliant erudition. Some of the nation's leading intellects, like Jean-Paul Sartre, began their intellectual careers as *lycée* professors (*not* teachers). The tradition of the *lycée* remains a strong one to this day, but after the Liberation secondary education in France began to evolve more along the lines of the American high school. The minimum school-leaving age was gradually raised from age fourteen to sixteen by the 1960s. This reform, plus the creation of a new type of comprehensive school, the *collège*, in 1963, helped to democratise secondary education to a certain extent. Although many *lycées* retained an upper-class character, it was no longer rare to see workers' children in secondary schools. By the 1960s French universities were experiencing the same rapid expansion as the secondary schools, with resulting stresses and strains that fuelled the explosion of May 1968.

The expansion of secondary education and the universities created the basis for a large youth culture in postwar France. Although less radically than in Britain or America, French young people also began to challenge the society of their elders in the 1950s and 1960s. Probably the first significant example of this was the *zazous* of the Occupation era, young Parisians whose resistance to Vichy assumed a cultural dimension, embracing jazz and other forms of avant-garde popular culture. In the late 1940s the vogue for existentialist philosophy turned the Left Bank neighbourhood of Saint-Germain-des-Prés into the privileged site of young rebels against the established order, whose berets, Gauloise cigarettes, love of jazz, and preference for extended stints in cafés inspired the Beatnik phenomenon that swept the world. A decade later rock music, to a large extent imported, triggered the development of a new form of youth culture. A June 1963 rock music broadcast in Paris attracted 150,000 dancing teenagers, loudly heralding the new youth culture and confirming the stardom of performers like Johnny Hallyday. Young people made important contributions to other art forms as well. Two of the most important innovations of the postwar era, the New Novel and cinema's New Wave, were pioneered by people in their twenties. In the countryside, the youth movement known as the Christian Agricultural Youth took the lead in dragging French farmers into the modern era.

Nonetheless, as with French women, the nation's youth seemed relatively quiescent during the 1950s and 1960s. Although young people represented not only the hope of the nation but also its new dynamism, they seemed largely content to follow the dictates of their parents. However, as the student uprisings of May 1968 would demonstrate, the new generation had its own ideas and, given the right circumstances, could act forcefully to make them heard. More generally, the mere demographic fact of a massive, new, young population reshaped postwar French society, sometimes in unexpected ways. The long period of prosperity created a new phenomenon in France – mass youth culture – one that would remain a permanent part of the national landscape.

Foreigners, especially immigrant workers, were a third group that made a major impact on French society during the postwar era. France has a long tradition of receiving newcomers from other lands, so that a sizeable percentage of French people today can point to foreign ancestors. During the 1920s France took in more immigrants than any other nation in the world. Their reception was not always easy, however. The French have frequently shown themselves to be hostile towards outsiders, and this hostility turned deadly during the 1930s and 1940s. Most foreigners in France were sent packing during the Depression and the Occupation, but the immigrant presence was never completely eradicated (many members of the Resistance, for example, were foreigners, especially anti-fascist Italians and Spaniards).

During the postwar years foreigners meant foreign workers above all, people who chose to come to France from elsewhere in search of better jobs and economic opportunity. After the Liberation it became clear to French policy-makers that a strong economic revival depended in part on an abundant supply of labour, yet thanks to low interwar birth rates this could not be found among the French people alone. Experts debated whether or not immigration should be a temporary or permanent phenomenon: economists like Jean Monnet tended to favour the former perspective, whereas demographers viewed immigration as a permanent way of boosting the French population. But all sides agreed it was necessary. In November 1945 the government established the National Immigration Office, and charged it with recruiting foreign workers for France's industries. During the *trentes glorieuses*, therefore, immigrant labourers came to France as much-desired guests of government and industry. As a result of these policies, the number of foreigners in France doubled from 1.7 million in 1946 to 3.4 million in 1975, constituting by the latter date 6.5 per cent of the nation's population.

Who were these strangers from a distant shore, and how did they live in France? They came, like most immigrants to France in earlier eras, primarily from other European nations: 89 per cent were of European origin in 1946, declining to 61 per cent by 1975. Although countries like Belgium and Poland continued to furnish important contingents, the majority came from the Mediterranean: Italy, Spain, and especially Portugal sent migrants year after year in search of a better life in France. By 1975 there were 758,000 Portuguese in France, constituting the single largest group of foreigners in the nation. France also began to attract a substantial number of non-European immigrant workers, especially from Algeria and other parts of North Africa. The immigrants were overwhelmingly young and middle-aged men, either bachelors or married men who had left their wives and children behind while they went to work in France. They worked in a variety of jobs, but generally those requiring low skill levels and offering low wages. Many worked in the nationalised auto and steel industries, operating heavy machinery and working on assembly lines. By 1969 two out of every five Renault employees was an immigrant. Foreign labourers also worked in the construction industry, the hotel and restaurant trade, and many other sectors of the economy. By the 1960s the Algerian or African immigrant sweeping the streets had become one of the classic sights of Paris.

For most foreign workers, life in France meant being relegated to the margins of French society. Most knew little or no French when they arrived, and usually lacked the opportunities to learn more than the bare minimum necessary for survival. At work they were generally assigned to segregated workspaces along with other immigrants, so that getting to know French people did not happen easily. Workplace isolation was reinforced by segregated, poor-quality housing. As with jobs, immigrant workers generally got the worst lodgings in France. Some lived in urban slum districts in large cities, and many more inhabited squalid shanty towns in the suburbs, living in shacks hastily built during the early 1950s to accommodate them. By the late 1950s the so-called *bidonvilles*, huts often built out of tin or cardboard, had become a national scandal, and most immigrant workers were moved to the new public housing projects during the 1960s. Yet as immigrants moved in French families often moved out and public authorities turned a blind eye to the gradual deterioration of much public housing into new slums. In addition, there was little provision for any kind of a social or cultural life for France's immigrant workers, so that once they left work in the evening they often had no public place to go beyond bars and cafés. Many ended up hanging out at train stations on Sundays, for lack of any better type of public life.

French attitudes towards immigrants were largely neutral during the 1950s and 1960s. The hostility of earlier periods did not entirely disappear, and many French citizens looked upon these outsiders with suspicion, or at least believed that they would always be different, a group apart. However, such antagonism was tempered by the strong economy and the feeling that immigrant workers posed no real threat to the nation. Some even recognised the key role these foreigners played in the economic dynamism of the era. Moreover, the fact that most immigrants were white Europeans also acted in their favour. In 1951, for example, an opinion poll revealed that the French had developed a hierarchy of ethnic and national preferences when it came to immigrant workers. Italians and Belgians received the most favourable reactions, then central and eastern Europeans. North Africans were viewed with the greatest hostility. The fact that during the postwar era immigrant workers were overwhelmingly invited to France by industry and government made little difference to French popular opinions of them.

It was therefore one of the paradoxes of France's postwar prosperity that it was to an important extent dependent upon a group of people who shared little of its fruits. Such a disparity flew in the face of Resistance ideals of social equality, one that could be easily ignored as long as the immigrant workers themselves remained largely unseen and unheard by most French people. Moreover, in one crucial aspect this disparity increased during the 1960s. As Italy, Spain, and Portugal experienced their own economic booms, the number of migrants from those countries began to decline, increasingly replaced by non-whites from Africa and the Caribbean. Whereas non-Europeans constituted only 12 per cent of immigrants in 1946, they accounted for 23 per cent in 1968 and 39 per cent by 1975. Quietly, gradually, the issue of immigration was turning into one of race, one that would loom much larger once the postwar good times came to an end.

In general, then, the economic boom transformed French society, but the changes were not immediately recognisable. The patriarchal double standard remained firmly in place, and while young people became more of a distinct subculture, in many ways they kept to the ways of their parents. The nation absorbed an unprecedented number of foreigners, but to a large extent they were invisible to the society as a whole. Yet if these changes were not as evident as the massive new housing projects in French suburbs, or the thousands of new cars on new highways, they were every bit as profound and important. The late 1960s and 1970s would show more clearly just how much the long era of postwar prosperity had transformed French society.

AMERICA AND THE THREAT OF 'COCA-COLONIZATION'

No other nation loomed larger in France's postwar imagination than the United States of America. Liberated with the help of American military might, restored to prosperity with American financial aid, France existed very much in the US orbit during the postwar years. Yet American dominance was not only military and economic, but also cultural. Throughout the twentieth century America had symbolised prosperous consumer society and the future in general, so much so that modernisation was often referred to as Americanisation. Many French wondered if the transformations reshaping their nation during the *trente glorieuses* were in fact making France into a carbon copy of their great overseas ally. Some looked at such a prospect with hope and satisfaction, others with horror, but few who thought about the broader ramifications of the economic boom could avoid trans-Atlantic comparisons. In the postwar era, therefore, French views of the United States reflected French concerns about the impact of good times on the national character.

One of the first instances of this concern was the strange controversy over the sale and marketing of Coca-Cola in France. America's 'national beverage' had been sold there since 1919, but only after 1945 did the Coca-Cola company launch a major drive to market its product overseas. However, Coke's plans to build a bottling plant in Marseilles and step up sales in France soon provoked a firestorm of protest, especially in the wake of rumours that Coke advertisements would be placed on the walls of Notre Dame cathedral. The French Communists took the lead, charging that American capitalism was trying to 'Coca-Colonize' their nation. They received powerful support from France's highly organised wine industry, which, along with other beverage manufacturers, feared such overseas competition. In 1949, after the government had tried to block Coke sales, the National Assembly took up the issue, passing a bill empowering the minister of public health to ban non-alcoholic beverages deemed a health danger. The debate provoked an uproar in both France and America, because it challenged not just one American company but the entire post-war economic and cultural relationship between the two nations. As *Le Monde* put it, 'What the French criticize is less Coca-Cola than its orchestration, less the drink itself, than the civilization – or as they like to say, the style of life – of which it is the symbol' (Kuisel, 1993: 65). In other words, the battle between wine and Coke was a struggle between French and American culture. Nonetheless, after the parliamentary debate the furore soon died down, and Coca-Cola went on sale in France after all. Eventually even the Communist daily newspaper *L'Humanité* would carry its advertisements.

Coca-Cola's victory presaged things to come, for to a significant extent France's postwar consumer revolution was based on the importation of American products. Brand names like Levi-Strauss, Marlboro, Quaker Oats and Tide now became familiar to French consumers. By the 1960s, as Richard Kuisel has put it, 'A Frenchman could now stay at a Hilton hotel in a room cooled by a Honeywell air conditioner and rent a car from Hertz' (Kuisel, 1993: 151). A popular 1958 French film, *La belle Américaine*, por-trayed the impact of a big American car (not a beautiful woman) on a working-class French neighbourhood. The ultimate symbol of this product invasion was the opening of France's first McDonald's in the late 1960s. French culture in particular seemed under siege by an army of American consumer goods. Thanks in part to postwar economic negotiations, Holly-wood movies quickly secured a stronghold in national cinemas. French cafés, sacrosanct sites of both urban and village culture, were invaded by *les flippers*, pinball machines. The 1960s also witnessed the birth of that dreaded cultural hybrid, Franglais, as French advertisers and ordinary citizens alike increasingly spiced up their French with hip terms borrowed from overseas.

The spectre of cultural Americanization soon became a major preoccupation of French intellectuals, especially those Parisian writers and thinkers centred in Saint-Germain-des-Prés. The Paris intellectual Left remained the most important stronghold of the spirit of the Resistance during the 1940s and 1950s, and one of the central tenets of this subculture was a critical attitude towards the United States. This was true both of those who belonged to, or sympathised with, the Communist Party, and those who pursued an ideological course independent of both superpowers. The concerns expressed by French intellectuals with consumer culture and Americanization paralleled and reinforced their fears of America's military and economic dominance of Europe.

Leftist writers and professors criticised the United States on several fronts. America was portrayed as a land without real culture (except that imported from Europe). Instead of valuing affairs of the mind and the spirit, it gloried in crass materialism. As the poet Louis Aragon, the Communist Party's leading intellectual, put it, 'The Yankee ... substitutes the machine for the poet, Coca-Cola for poetry ... the mass-manufactured car for the genius, the Ford for Victor Hugo!' (Kuisel, 1993: 41). In short, America was a land that possessed unparalleled wealth but no soul. Parisian intellectuals also criticised American conformism, seeing the nation as a place that emphasised sameness and agreement over diversity and the play of many different opinions. Capitalist standardisation in the United States meant that, coast to coast, one could find the same chain stores, the same movies, the same ideas. For all their vaunted freedom to choose, Americans seemed bent upon always making the same choices. Finally, many considered American confidence in the superiority of their way of life to be unbridled arrogance, both irritating and rooted in wilful ignorance about the rest of the world.

Yet this is not the whole story, for some aspects of American culture also attracted French intellectuals. Many admired America's dynamism, its willingness to break with the past and embrace the new, and even its brutal honesty. France has had a long love–hate relationship with the United States, based on similarities as well as differences between the two nations, and probably at no time was this ambiguity more sharply felt than during the postwar years. One interesting example of this is the French attitude towards African Americans. Paris during the 1950s and 1960s played host to a flourishing community of black expatriates from the USA, a community made very welcome in France precisely because blacks represented both positive and negative extremes of American life. The French had long viewed American racism as one of the worst sins of their trans-Atlantic ally, those on the Left in particular using it to refute notions of American superiority. At the same time many French people loved jazz and regarded it as one of the few unique cultural products to come out of the United States. During the 1950s and 1960s Saint-Germain-des-Prés itself was home to several jazz clubs, many of which featured African American expatriate musicians. This combination of attraction to American popular culture and disdain for American politics in a broader sense often characterised the reactions of Parisian intellectuals, and French people in general, to the United States.

At bottom, what worried French intellectuals and many others about American culture was the idea that economic modernisation might turn France into its mirror image. Would prosperity undermine the rich legacy of French culture, turning the nation into a homogeneous landscape of fast-food outlets and dime-store mystery novels? Would French identity survive 'Americanization'? Ultimately, the issue was not the United States, but rather consumer culture, and while critics of shallow materialism certainly had a point, it was hard to argue convincingly that poverty was preferable to prosperity. Moreover, French culture was far too deeply rooted to disappear under the onslaught of mass-produced goods. French life did change with the consumer revolution, but it remained uniquely French. For example, the French did not simply buy American blue jeans, but also made their own, high fashion version, which they were exporting to Americans by the 1970s. French television programming was distinctly more intellectual than its American equivalents. Ultimately, the postwar economic boom did create some trans-Atlantic similarities, but France did not 'Americanize', finding instead its own ways to embrace consumer culture.

The France that most of us are familiar with today came into being during the 1950s and 1960s. Even something as prototypically French as the *baguette*, that long skinny loaf of white bread so intriguing to tourists, only became common in the postwar years. For the most part, the nation's economic boom must be considered a roaring success. It brought to many people a standard of living undreamed of by their grandparents, and seemed to banish social evils like hunger and chronic unemployment. Consumerism may have had its aesthetic and spiritual disadvantages, but most French people enjoyed their better housing, new cars and televisions very much indeed. A society full of healthy babies and confident families was, after all, a political goal and a big part of what the Resistance had hoped to achieve.

But all was not perfect in postwar France. The review of social conditions has shown that prosperity did not reach everyone in the country equally, nor did it resolve all the problems of those who did benefit. The next chapter will consider a much less positive part of postwar French history, relations with the nation's overseas colonies. The empire may have seemed far removed from the day-to-day concerns of metropolitan France, yet in fact the turmoil going on there both mirrored and affected life in the homeland. Like the situation of immigrant workers in France, the trauma of imperial decolonisation revealed fundamental differences about what it meant to be French in the modern era.

CHAPTER FOUR

FROM DECOLONISATION TO NEO-COLONIALISM

One of the great scenes from the classic 1942 film *Casablanca*, set in wartime Morocco, shows a musical duel between German soldiers singing *Watch on the Rhine* and French supporters of de Gaulle and the Resistance singing *The Marseillaise*. This 'battle of the bands', and the film in general, provides a stirring, if not always accurate, account of the struggle between Vichy and Free French forces in French North Africa during the Second World War. It does not seem to have occurred to Hollywood, nor to many French people, that there was another perspective to consider, that of the Moroccans themselves. The suggestion that they might wish to be ruled by neither side in France's civil war never appears in the movie *Casablanca*. However, in the real-life Morocco ideas of autonomy, even independence, had already gained a foothold, and would shake the empire to its foundations once the war ended.

In 1945 France possessed one of the greatest colonial empires in the history of the world, second only to that of the United Kingdom. Twenty years later this global phenomenon had all but vanished, leaving only a few scattered island possessions in the Americas and the Indian Ocean. The history of the decolonisation of the French empire is central to the history of postwar France, and in contrast to the saga of the nation's economic revival, it is generally a tragic tale from the French perspective. Much more so than Britain, France bitterly resisted the winds of independence sweeping through Europe's African and Asian colonies after the Second World War, as a result becoming embroiled in bloody colonial wars for sixteen years non-stop. Before the French finally bowed to the inevitable, hundreds of thousands of lives would be needlessly sacrificed.

Many reasons explain France's futile attempt to preserve colonial mastery, but at the base of this tragedy lay the contradiction between universalism and nationalism central to French life since the great Revolution. While the protagonists of 1789 had proclaimed liberty, equality and fraternity to be rights merited by all humanity, they generally failed to separate the universal aspects of their Revolution from what was purely

French. Napoleon liberated the peoples of Europe from feudalism by imposing upon them French law and political practices, for example. For many French men and women in the modern era to be civilised meant to adopt French culture and beliefs. By the beginning of the twentieth century France had paradoxically become a Republican empire, a nation founded upon the principle of universal citizenship that nonetheless ruled millions of colonial subjects. The resistance against Nazism and Vichy renewed the national commitment to the liberationist values of the Revolution, yet it did not always apply this commitment to those whose idea of liberation meant liberation from France. This was especially ironic because, in calling for independence from France, many of the nationalist rebels in postwar Indochina, Algeria and other colonies based their appeal squarely upon the universalist principles of the French Revolution and the Resistance, turning their colonisers' own rhetoric and beliefs against them.

At no time in the history of modern France was this contradiction between universalism and French patriotism more intensely evident than during the postwar years of decolonisation. This paradox explains why events occurring in an overseas empire loomed so large in the history of the metropole. In spite of the many difficulties and failings of the Fourth Republic, it was its failed colonial policy that destroyed it and inaugurated the Fifth Republic. The empire may have been marginal to France geographically, but it was central to French politics and culture in the decades after the Second World War.

FRANCE AND ITS EMPIRE IN 1945

When war began in 1939 the French possessed a colonial empire that was the envy of many nations. The French flag flew over large stretches of west, north and central Africa, numerous islands in the Pacific and Caribbean, and Indochina in Southeast Asia. Although not as important to national identity as was the British empire to that of the English, during the interwar years France's colonies had begun to play an important role in the nation's consciousness. During the First World War the French had imported hundreds of thousands of colonial subjects to fight and labour in the metropole, representing the first time in France's history that a large non-white population had set foot on its soil. Their contribution to the victory of 1918, plus the continued threat from a resentful (not to mention larger and more powerful Germany), led many to speak of France as a 'nation of 100 million Frenchmen'. Germany might have a larger population, but France's empire could more than compensate for the economic and military weaknesses of the metropole. The increased awareness of the empire's usefulness interacted with a new appreciation of colonial cultures and exoticism. Several national fairs gave prominent display to imperial themes, notably the 1931 Paris Colonial Exposition. Newspapers, movies and literature devoted extensive coverage to the problems and attractions of empire. Even the vogue for African American music and performance arose in part from this fascination with empire: in her many stage and film performances, for example, Josephine Baker usually played a young woman from the colonies.

The Second World War underscored the lessons of the First about the importance of the empire to France's national identity, indeed national survival. Although most of the colonies, like the metropole, initially rallied to Vichy in 1940, there were some exceptions, including New Caledonia, Tahiti and French Equatorial Africa. More importantly, de Gaulle's Free French scored their first successes in the empire, long before their triumphal return to Paris in 1944. North Africa in particular witnessed a struggle between Vichy and Free French forces, the latter gaining the upper hand by 1943 in the wake of the Allied landings there. De Gaulle first raised the flag of Free France in the colonies, not the metropole. Moreover, a large percentage of the soldiers who fought with de Gaulle's forces were colonial subjects, including 300,000 North African Arabs. The empire may have contributed to the French victory in the First World War, but to a much greater extent in the Second World War the colonies liberated the metropole.

In spite of this, most French people had paid relatively little attention to the empire during the war, preoccupied with their own tragic domestic concerns. Even the role of colonial subjects in the Free French was generally ignored by a nation bent on believing that Frenchmen, not outsiders, had liberated France. Nonetheless, once the war was over the dominant figures in French politics and public life agreed that France must maintain her colonial empire. Unlike Britain, which recognised the winds of change and peacefully granted independence to the crown jewel of its empire, India, in 1947, the French struggled to hang on to an increasingly anachronistic colonial dominance. Although France had ultimately won the Second World War, it had been defeated and occupied for four years by Nazi Germany, a defeat that constituted a bitter humiliation for the French people. Many felt that the nation could only restore its status as a great power if it retained its world empire. The bipolar era of superpower dominance after 1945 reinforced the importance of colonial possessions if France was to remain anything more than a second-rate European nation, under the control of either Washington or Moscow. Thus the idea, so dear to the Resistance, of Europe as an alternative to both American capitalism and Soviet Communism fed into a determination to preserve the French empire. More particularly, both the military and France's powerful colonial lobby were determined to keep the empire French no matter what, and agitated tirelessly to ensure that outcome. Finally, many believed that the raw materials and the markets of the colonies were vital to the nation's economic recovery. The empire had provided a certain cushion during the Depression, and hopefully would do so again after the war.

For all these reasons, therefore, the French found it much more difficult than the British to accept the end of formal empire gracefully after 1945. But if the war had shown the value of the colonies to France, it had also given many colonial subjects a new perspective on their relations with the mother country. Japan's victories in East Asia over the European imperial powers pointedly demonstrated that whites could be defeated by soldiers of colour, a lesson not lost on many Indochinese in particular. The defeat and occupation of France by Germany showed the nation's vulnerability and caused it to lose prestige in the eyes of its colonial subjects. At the same time, the actions of France's allies also called into question the solidity of its imperial mission. When Allied forces landed in North Africa in 1943 they brought with them copies, in Arabic, of the Atlantic Charter, a document which called for the self-determination of all peoples, and distributed them to local populations. In January 1943, American President Franklin Delano Roosevelt met with the Sultan of Morocco and proclaimed his country's support for Morocco's right to decide its own future. In the Pacific, large sections of Tahiti and New Caledonia were 'occupied' by American troops, whose wealth and technological sophistication often put the local French elites to shame. Most dramatically, in 1941, the Free French granted independence to the League of Nations mandate of Syria and Lebanon, largely due to British pressure. Although full independence was not achieved until 1946, the French imperial presence there effectively ended during the war.

Colonial intellectual and political leaders reacted to these developments by stepping up the pressure for self-rule. In March 1943, Algerian nationalists issued a manifesto demanding autonomy for their nation. As the defeat of Japan drew near, the Communist Viet Minh moved into high gear in Indochina, eventually proclaiming an independent state in September 1945. A tragic incident in Algeria showed clearly, for those with eyes to see, that the postwar era would not bring a simple restoration of French colonialism. In the town of Sétif, villagers gathered on 8 May 1945 to celebrate the victory in Europe. The occasion turned violent when police attacked nationalists protesting about the recent deportation of their leader Messali Hadj and the French administration in general. The riots prompted a Muslim insurrection in the area, during which some 100 Europeans were killed. The French responded by sending in thousands of troops and attacking Arab villages from the air. Ultimately, the Muslim death toll at Sétif was estimated to range from 8,000 to 45,000. The war was over, but a new war had begun.

The French were not completely oblivious to such pressures, but tended to think in terms of reforming colonialism, not abolishing it. A congress on the postwar empire held by the Free French in Brazzaville at the beginning of 1944 concluded that colonial subjects deserved greater rights, but that the colonies were not yet ready for independence. The formal establishment of the Fourth Republic in 1946 included major new legislation concerning the empire. A series of laws made all colonial subjects citizens (though not equal to metropolitan French citizens), abolished forced labour, granted departmental status to the colonies of Martinique, Guadeloupe, French Guiana and Réunion, and created the French Union to replace the old empire. These reforms were important, but they remained just that, reforms. France continued to control the destiny of its overseas possessions, and racial hierarchies continued to place whites in a superior political and economic position to non-whites. At a time when more and more voices were challenging colonialism as a whole, these reforms represented a classic case of too little, too late. France's refusal to go further than that in re-thinking its imperial mission thus set the stage for the bloody drama of decolonisation over the next two decades.

THE WAR IN INDOCHINA

Indochina, consisting of the modern nations of Vietnam, Cambodia and Laos, was France's only significant colony in East Asia, and one of its great imperial possessions. Throughout the empire, Indochina also proved to be one of the colonies most resistant to French control. In part this arose from the area's pre-colonial history. For centuries before the arrival of the French, the Chinese had dominated Indochina, shaping its culture but also prompting the rise of nationalist resentment. Vietnam in particular, the largest and most important nation in Indochina, had a long history of resistance to the Chinese, so that much of Vietnamese national identity centred around struggles for national integrity and against foreign invaders. When the French invaded in the 1880s, in response to the decline of effective Chinese control of Indochina, they confronted a people with a strong tradition of resistance, so much so that even after formal conquest wars of 'pacification' continued for decades.

The strength of Indochinese resistance was due not just to tradition, but also to the harsh conditions imposed upon them by French imperialism. French rule featured both wanton physical brutality and systematic economic exploitation. The colonisers developed the region's infrastructure, building harbours, railways, bridges and canals, to promote trade with the metropole, and methodically allowed French settlers to appropriate village lands and turn them into plantations. Indochinese peasants were stripped of their lands and forced into working on rubber plantations and mines in situations little different from slavery. As a result, the era of French rule in

Indochina saw a precipitous drop in local living standards. This harsh exploitation helped feed the fires of nationalism in Indochina during the early twentieth century. Organised political resistance to French rule was most prominent in Vietnam, and began with that nation's urban, Westernised elite youth. These were men and women who had learned about French culture and ideas of universal liberty, so the contradiction between those ideas and French treatment of colonial subjects was all the more galling. They founded a variety of nationalist political movements, as well as a small but influential Communist party, during the 1920s, and managed to stage a series of major revolts against French rule in 1930–31. These were harshly repressed by the French, forcing the anti-colonial movement into a clandestine campaign. Gradually, during the 1930s, the Communists, under the leadership of Ho Chi Minh, became the leading force in the struggle for the liberation of Indochina.

The fall of France in 1940, and the invasion of the colony by Japanese troops, created a complex new situation in French Indochina. A French government allied with Vichy remained in control, but it became increasingly clear that Japan held the upper hand. The Indochinese Communists responded in 1941 by declaring war against both the French and the Japanese, founding a new guerrilla army, the Viet Minh. The Viet Minh sought to rally all nationalists to its cause and launched frequent, daring attacks against Japanese troops. In March 1945 the Japanese forcibly deposed the French government of Indochina, arresting many French officials and civilians, and proclaimed the nations of Indochina independent under puppet emperor Bao Dai. After the Japanese surrender in August, Bao Dai's government collapsed and the Viet Minh occupied northern Vietnam. At the beginning of September British troops landed in southern Vietnam, paving the way for the return of French forces there. By the end of 1945, therefore, Indochina was effectively divided between the Viet Minh in north Vietnam and the French in south Vietnam, Laos and Cambodia.

1946 saw a complex series of negotiations between the French and the Viet Minh that ultimately collapsed, leading to war between the two sides. French opinion about the future of French Indochina was divided: some were willing to recognise Viet Minh control of north Vietnam, while reasserting French mastery of the rest of Indochina. This faction had some success at first, so that in March 1946 de Gaulle's government made vague promises about granting independence to Vietnam, or at least autonomy within the French Union. A strong coalition of colonial officials, known as the 'Saigon clique', opposed any such concessions, however, and was able to win support in key military and diplomatic circles. After the suspension of negotiations in June, the French government resolved to oppose the Viet Minh and retake northern Vietnam by force if necessary. In November France ordered the Viet Minh to evacuate the main port city of Haiphong.

When the latter failed to do so, the French Navy bombarded the city, killing over 6,000 people. The French Army then landed in force, capturing the capital city, Hanoi, by February 1947, and triggering guerrilla resistance by the Viet Minh throughout the north.

Thus began the French war in Indochina, a war which not only corresponded to the pattern of other colonial conflicts but also set the mould for America's later war in Vietnam. French forces succeeded in quickly taking control of major population centres in the north. They had the advantage of superior firepower, especially aviation and warships, and a larger army. However, in waging war against the Viet Minh the French also had to contend with some serious problems. The Viet Minh troops were much better entrenched, and when the French invaded they were able to withdraw to strongholds in the north that their enemies could not overcome. France also had to deal with the logistics nightmare of supplying a war fought several thousand miles from the metropole, at a time when the French economy was just recovering from the Second World War.

French public opinion did not support the war unanimously. The French Communists sharply opposed it, and their opposition had much to do with the collapse of Tripartism. Many others saw the conflict as one fought to benefit a small number of colonialists, notably the French-owned Bank of Indochina. Indochina was far away, and the majority of 'French' forces there were either colonial subjects or foreigners (including a number of Germans in the Foreign Legion). As a result, the average French person did not see the Indochina war as particularly important. In Indochina itself, by contrast, the Viet Minh were able to win the allegiance of the clear majority of the local population. Not only did they benefit from strong anti-colonial sentiments, but also won popular support thanks to their leading role in the struggle against Japan. In particular, the French made the mistake of seriously underestimating Viet Minh support in southern Vietnam. Like the Resistance in France, the Viet Minh in Indochina stood for anti-fascism as both nationalism and social change. The Viet Minh also terrorised those Indochinese who opposed them, creating another means of rallying support. As a result, the French may have controlled the cities and the villages by day, but the Viet Minh ruled by night.

A major turning point in the war occurred with the victory of the Communists in China, in October 1949. Mao Zedong's triumph gave the Viet Minh somewhat better access to supplies and friendly territory at their backs, although in reality the Chinese Communists did relatively little to aid their Vietnamese colleagues. More significantly, the spectre of Asian Communism on the march helped transform the French war from a colonial to an ideological one. The French forces in Indochina had long portrayed their battle as one against Communism, especially after the collapse of Tripartism at home in 1947. With the Communist takeover of China and the

start of the Korean War the following year, they could now more convincingly portray their struggle as one more front in the Cold War. The
increasingly anti-Communist nature of the Indochina conflict not only
convinced Emperor Bao Dai to ally with the French, but more importantly
persuaded the United States to support French efforts there. Initially hostile
to European postwar efforts to preserve empire, by the early 1950s
American policy-makers had concluded that imperialism was preferable to
Soviet control. Consequently, Washington began to contribute substantial
financial aid to the French in Indochina. These developments also helped
change French policies so that more and more they were fighting not to
keep Indochina as a formal colony, but rather to assure that an independent
Vietnam was ruled by a non-Communist, pro-French regime.

In spite of this shift in orientation, however, the French steadily lost
ground in Indochina. Most Indochinese continued to view the conflict as
primarily a colonial war and Bao Dai as a French puppet. As the war
escalated, France committed more and more troops to the area, over
300,000 by 1953. This made the war more of a financial burden than ever,
one bearable only because America was now paying the lion's share of
expenses. In Indochina the French continued to lose ground in the countryside, while more and more recruits flocked to the Viet Minh, enabling them
to move gradually from guerrilla to regular warfare. The end came in May
1954, when, after a five-month battle, the French Army was roundly
defeated at the fortress of Dien Bien Phu. This military disaster caused the
collapse of the French government. A new government was formed by
Pierre Mendes-France, a centrist politician who had long preached a
negotiated settlement in Indochina. Under his leadership France went to the
peace negotiations at Geneva in July 1954, there recognising the independence of Indochina. Vietnam was to be divided temporarily at the 17th
parallel between the governments of Ho Chi Minh and Bao Dai, pending
national elections for a unified Vietnamese government. These elections
were never held and the country remained divided, eventually paving the
way for the far more devastating American war in Vietnam. For the first
time in over seventy years, the Tricolour flag no longer flew over French
territory in East Asia.

ALGERIA AND THE COLLAPSE OF THE FOURTH REPUBLIC

By the time France signed the Geneva Accords in 1954 the empire had been
challenged from several quarters. In 1945 France had formally ceded control of its concessions in several Chinese cities to that nation's government,
and by 1954 would grant to India sovereignty over the French enclave of
Pondichéry. In March 1947 nationalists in the island kingdom of Madagascar staged an armed uprising against France, motivated by widespread

discontent with crop requisitions and forced labour imposed during the war. The insurrection spread rapidly, rebels attacking French military outposts and civilians alike. The French soon gained the upper hand, however, and succeeded in wiping out the last resistance by the end of 1948. Nearly 90,000 Malagasy died in the conflict, and the colony did not win its independence until 1960.

The first decade after the Liberation also saw France's two North African protectorates, Morocco and Tunisia, win their independence. Both nations had been sites of fighting between Allied and Axis forces during the war, and both had powerful independence movements. In Morocco, the Independence Party succeeded in winning the allegiance of the sultan. When the French responded by deposing him in 1953, a cycle of riots and repression plunged the colony into turmoil until Paris finally recognised the futility of the situation and surrendered its rule over Morocco in 1956. Events in Tunisia followed a similar pattern. After its reforms failed to mollify nationalists, France arrested the leader of the independence movement, Habib Bourguiba, thereby further radicalising the situation. The French soon saw the errors of this approach and granted independence to Tunisia a few days after Morocco. France's recent loss of Indochina played no small role in teaching French leaders that relations with the empire would have to change dramatically if the nation was to preserve any influence there in the future.

It was the great tragedy of postwar French decolonisation that such wisdom was not applied to Algeria. Instead, France's largest North African territory became the site of an eight-year brutal conflict, not only the most bitter experienced by the French empire after the war, but quite possibly the worst of all cases of European decolonisation in the mid-twentieth century. Even more than in Indochina, the French went into the Algerian war determined to hang on to this vestige of empire, only giving up when the struggle threatened the well-being of not only Algeria but France as well. Several reasons explain the French resolve to keep Algeria French until the bitter end. Algeria was technically not a colony at all, but legally an integral part of France, three overseas departments. Unlike Indochina, Algeria was very close to the metropole; Marseilles, France's great Mediterranean port, was just as close to Algiers as it was to Paris. Perhaps most important of all, roughly 10 per cent, or 1 million people, of the Algerian population consisted of French settlers. These individuals, often people from other parts of Europe who had become French by settling in Algeria, lived a privileged existence compared to the Muslim population, and were adamant in their desire that Algeria remain a part of France. In addition, many soldiers and officers in the French military felt they had been betrayed by the politicians into losing Indochina, and were determined that this history should not repeat itself in North Africa.

As Sétif made clear in 1945, however, postwar Algeria was a powder keg, because the indigenous population had its own ideas about whether or not their country should remain part of France. The French made minor legislative reforms in the wake of Sétif, but these small changes continued to ensure settler control of the territory. One result was an increased radicalisation of the Algerian nationalist movement. Whereas before the Second World War most nationalist leaders had called for autonomy and continued association with France, now demands for outright independence emerged as the dominant theme of the movement. By 1954, inspired both by the victory of the Viet Minh and the rapid evolution of both Morocco and Tunisia toward independence, Algerian nationalists were ready to make their move. They organised an umbrella group, the National Liberation Front (FLN) to spearhead the struggle for liberation. On 31 October 1954 the FLN issued a manifesto proclaiming the independence of Algeria, and the next day launched a series of armed uprisings throughout the country, timed to coincide with the French holiday of All Saints' Day.

To a much greater extent than the war in Indochina, the Algerian war was as much a political as a military conflict. The FLN was extremely small in 1954, counting little more than 1,000 members, not all of whom were even armed. The French responded sharply to the 1 November attacks against army posts, sending in 20,000 troops to crush the rebellion. They succeeded in quickly capturing much of the FLN leadership, leaving the organisation weakened and divided by the start of 1955. Because of this weakness, the FLN decided to employ terror as a military and political weapon, not only against other Algerians to enforce compliance with FLN policies (such as a ban on smoking and alcohol), but also against French settlers, especially isolated farmers. The French responded in kind, so that the war soon degenerated into a vicious cycle of terror and counter-terror, in which no man, woman or child was safe. In June 1955, for example, the FLN massacred over 100 French civilians in the town of Phillippeville, going so far as to slaughter infants and disembowel women. French soldiers and armed settler vigilantes reacted with an orgy of violence, killing up to 12,000 Arab civilians. Phillippeville hardened opinions on both sides and made a compromise solution that much less likely. Most French people believed Algeria should remain part of the nation, and reacted to the massacre by supporting increased repression there. The government began a massive mobilisation of French draftees for the war. At the same time, Phillippeville was a major shot in the arm for the FLN, bringing it much needed support and recruits.

In 1956 the French Army began to call the shots in the Algerian war. The size of French forces increased to 390,000 by August. Moreover, in March, the Socialist government in Paris voted a Special Powers law for Algeria, declaring a state of emergency and giving the Army a free hand there. Over the next few years the Army, under the leadership of Generals Raoul Salan and Jacques Massu, pursued a policy of harsh repression, brutality and torture. Airborne paratroopers, soldiers who symbolised a kind of ascetic military romanticism and adventurism, played a key role in Army strategy. The Army sought to isolate the FLN by relocating entire Muslim villages, as well as building electrified fences along Algeria's borders with Tunisia and Morocco. Most notoriously, it freely employed torture to infiltrate FLN networks and break the back of the movement. The French victory over the FLN in the Battle of Algiers was a case in point. The battle began in September 1956 when FLN women planted bombs in cafés in European neighbourhoods. By December the FLN was staging an average of four bombings a day against the settler population in the capital city. The French Army responded brutally, forcing strikers to resume work at gun point, shooting those who resisted orders, and using electroshock, rape and other grisly techniques to ferret out information about the FLN's plans. On a military level such tactics were effective, bringing the FLN's offensive in Algiers to an end by October 1957.

Politically, however, the Army's repressive tactics merely underlined the bankruptcy of French policy in Algeria. The prospect of a Socialist government permitting a military reign of terror on what was technically French soil showed how little relevance Resistance notions of liberty had in France's colonies. A small anti-war movement, mostly the work of left-wing Parisian intellectuals, began to develop. Early in 1955 the writer Claude Bourdet published an article entitled 'Is there a Gestapo in Algeria?', attacking French brutality there. Much more important was Jean-Jacques Servan-Schreiber's 1957 memoir of his military service, *Lieutenant in Algeria*. Servan-Schreiber edited the influential magazine *L'Express*, and his words carried a lot of weight with French public opinion. The fact that, unlike Indochina, the Algerian war relied upon French draftees also helped to sow discontent, even producing a few anti-draft riots. Yet none of the parties of the Left, including the Communists, solidly backed the movement, and the majority of French people continued to support their government's war in Algeria. As Albert Camus, Nobel Prize winning author and Resistance veteran but also French settler from Algeria, put it, 'I believe in justice, but I would defend my mother before justice' (Gildea, 1996: 22).

This began to change in 1958, the year the colonial war in Algeria came home to metropolitan France. In that year the strains of the war finally pushed the tottering Fourth Republic over the brink, causing a crisis of the regime which the French only resolved by founding a new republic and bringing Charles de Gaulle back to power. By 1958 the weaknesses of the Fourth Republic's parliamentary structure had become apparent, as coalition governments found themselves unable to do more than react to events in Algeria rather than taking forceful action. In April, a moderate coalition government collapsed, leaving the nation without an functioning regime for a full month. At the same time French settlers in Algeria began to grow restless, fearing that Paris would ultimately sell them out to the FLN. These tensions erupted on 13 May 1958 when settlers in Algiers first proclaimed a general strike, then a revolutionary seizure of power. On the same day Army paratroopers seized control of Corsica, raising the spectre of a military *coup d'état* in Paris itself. At this point all eyes turned to Charles de Gaulle, the saviour of French honour in 1940. Disgusted with the Fourth Republic, de Gaulle had dropped out of politics at the end of the 1940s, but as the crisis of the regime became manifest, he initiated feelers for a return to power. The crisis of May 1958 provided the opportunity he sought. After a complex series of negotiations de Gaulle agreed to take over the government. On 1 June the French parliament voted him prime minister, with special powers for six months. The parliament then disbanded, effectively ending the Fourth Republic. De Gaulle went on to draft the constitution for the new, Fifth Republic, a regime in which the president was far more powerful than in the Fourth Republic, and elected by national vote. In September French voters approved the new constitution by a favourable margin of 80 per cent. Just as the trauma of the Second World War had destroyed the Third Republic, so did the Algerian tragedy bring the Fourth to an inglorious end.

Immediately after his return to power de Gaulle flew to Algiers to assure settlers and their supporters in the Army that he understood their position. Yet de Gaulle did not embrace their insistence on French Algeria, understanding that the war could not be resolved by military means. Moreover, he saw clearly that unless the conflict was resolved, it posed a grave threat to French democracy and well-being. First on his agenda was assuring civilian control of the military, which he did by transferring Raoul Salan. De Gaulle then made his position clear in September 1959 by announcing support for the principle of Algerian self-determination, and shortly thereafter undertaking negotiations with the FLN. This was not at all to the liking of the settlers in Algeria, who felt personally betrayed by de Gaulle. They responded with a new uprising in Algiers in January 1960. This time, however, de Gaulle's mastery of the Army paid off, and French forces easily crushed the revolt. 1960 and 1961 witnessed increased violence not only in Algeria but in France as well. Discontented settlers and Army officers founded the Secret Army Organisation (OAS), which promptly launched a campaign of bombings and general terror against all those opposed to the idea of French Algeria. The OAS organised a military putsch in April 1961 in Algiers, led by four generals in open mutiny against de Gaulle's policies. The revolt failed when most French soldiers in Algeria remained loyal to Paris and arrested some of the mutineers.

By 1961 the violence had spread to France as well. Rumours constantly circulated around Paris about paratroopers landing to stage a military takeover of the government. The OAS, which by the end of the year was staging thousands of terror attacks each month in Algeria, also bombed the homes and offices of French liberals and Muslims in the metropole. In September it almost succeeded in assassinating de Gaulle himself in Paris. The FLN also stepped up its activities in France, mostly against dissident Algerians. It was not uncommon to see the bodies of dead Algerians floating down the Seine through Paris by this time. The French police reacted harshly to both groups, especially the FLN. In February Paris police attacked a leftist anti-OAS demonstration at the Charonne metro stop, killing eight people. Far worse was the repression of the October demonstration led by the Paris FLN, in which police massacred an estimated 200 individuals in the heart of the nation's capital. The interminable character of the war, and the spread of violence to the metropole, produced a fundamental shift in French public opinion about the war. As late as 1958 a clear majority of the nation wanted to keep Algeria French. Thereafter this changed rapidly, so that when, in January 1961, de Gaulle held a national referendum on the question of Algerian self-determination, 75 per cent voted in favour. Armed with this support de Gaulle pursued negotiations with the FLN, which in March 1962 produced the Evian Accords granting formal independence to Algeria. In spite of a last-minute campaign of terror by the OAS, the Algerian people overwhelmingly approved the agreement, and the Algerian war at long last came to an end. The war had cost roughly half a million lives, almost all Algerian Muslims, and led to the exodus of 1 million French settlers from their homes to France. France's long imperial presence in North Africa, home to the Foreign Legion and so many exoticist fantasies, had finally ceased to exist.

FROM EMPIRE TO FRANCOPHONE COMMUNITY

More than anyone else, Charles de Gaulle made the French understand that the days of formal European empire were no more. It was one of his greatest accomplishments, and perhaps it was inevitable that only the man who had symbolised the survival of France in its darkest hours could lead his people into the post-colonial era. Although Algeria was the most important symbol of the passing of the old French empire, de Gaulle also oversaw other aspects of this transition. He engineered the decolonisation of French sub-Saharan Africa and, perhaps more importantly, put in place structures that would govern France's future relations with its former colonies. Largely due to the work of de Gaulle and others in the 1960s, France was able to retain a large amount of influence in the old imperial areas, so much so that it is not quite accurate to speak simply of the end of empire. Rather, one must speak of a transformation of relations between metropole and colonies that left many of the old structures of domination in place. As a result, while achieving independence was undoubtedly very important for French colonies, their future association with France was often not so much post-colonial as neo-colonial.

Immediately upon assuming power in 1958, de Gaulle recognised that the Algerian conflict symbolised broader problems in the empire as a whole, and he moved forcefully to confront them. The nation had finally granted equal citizenship to all adults in the empire, but he decided to go further. As part of the constitution of the new Fifth Republic de Gaulle scrapped the old French Union in favour of a new Community, one to which France and its colonies would belong as equal members. In line with de Gaulle's love of referenda, all colonies would hold popular votes for either membership in the Community (in reality continued colonial status) or immediate independence. People were free to choose, with the catch that a vote for independence would mean the immediate cessation of all financial aid from the metropole. As a result, when the referendum was held on 28 September 1958 the overwhelming majority of colonial citizens voted for continued association with France. The one exception was the west African nation of Guinea, which opted for independence. The French showed their hostility to this move by not only stopping economic aid immediately, but also removing everything in the country that belonged to France, going so far as to unscrew light bulbs and rip telephones out of the wall.

By the late 1950s, thanks to the loss of Indochina and the turmoil in North Africa, the French empire essentially consisted of black Africa. France had held coastal outposts in Africa since the days of the trans-Atlantic slave trade, expanding into the interior in the mid and late nineteenth century. Compared to North Africa and Indochina, nationalism had been relatively slow to develop in the French colonies of sub-Saharan Africa, although French rule there was every bit as brutal and exploitative as elsewhere in the empire. This changed with the impact of the Second World War, so that by the late 1940s educated Africans were developing nationalist political parties, based first in urban areas but gradually enlisting the support of the peasantry as well. Leaders like Felix Houphouët-Boigny in the Ivory Coast and Leopold Sédar Senghor in Senegal began to press for autonomy within the empire, if not yet outright independence. By the time of the 1958 vote on the Community these parties were well established, leading the campaign for continued ties with France. Once the Community was formally established, however, its African constituents then began to push for formal independence, it being understood this time that such a step would not mean severing relations with France. De Gaulle and the French accepted this, so that in 1960 France formally ended its empire in sub-Saharan Africa, granting independence to no less than fourteen former colonies. As a result, 1960 became the great year of

African independence, symbolising the passing of French and European colonial rule in general.

With the granting of independence to the African colonies in 1960 the French empire essentially came to an end as a formal organisation. Yet in the forty years since the completion of decolonisation many economic, cultural and historical ties have continued to connect France with its former colonies. For one thing, the presence of several overseas departments and territories (DOM-TOMs) has perpetuated the dream of France as a global nation. Martinique, Guadeloupe and Guyana in the Caribbean, New Caledonia and Tahiti in the Pacific, and other smaller possessions have remained integral parts of the French nation. Their inhabitants are French citizens, many of whom routinely settle in the metropole, and their economies are closely tied to and subsidised by that of the home country. The DOM-TOMs have not always been perfectly happy under French rule, as the violent independence movement that erupted in New Caledonia during the 1980s and 1990s made clear. Nonetheless, little possibility exists that they will break away from France anytime soon.

One aspect of continuity between colonialism and neo-colonialism has been economic relations. As France modernised in the years after 1945, its trade with America and other European nations increased in value relative to its commerce with the empire. Nonetheless, trading relations with former colonies have remained important. Negotiations over independence usually included provisions for continued French access to local raw materials, such as natural gas in Algeria. Africa in particular has continued to provide many of the minerals, such as bauxite, manganese, cobalt, uranium and copper, that French industry needs. In return France has generally exported manufactured goods ranging from clothing to computers and armaments to its old imperial possessions. By the late 1980s, for example, France accounted for nearly half of Madagascar's exports, and supplied four-fifths of goods imported by Chad. France's balance of payments with former colonies have generally been positive, thus representing the continued benefits of colonialism for the French.

Yet the real importance to France of neo-colonial relations has been political and strategic rather than economic. With the signal exceptions of Algeria and especially Vietnam, the French have succeeded in keeping the former colonies loyal to their own foreign policies. Sub-Saharan Africa provides the clearest example of this. De Gaulle had granted independence in 1960 so quickly precisely because he wanted to ensure future friendly relations with the Africans, rather than the hostility that would certainly result from a bitter struggle against the inevitable. Moreover, African independence had the benefit of adding several new French allies to the United Nations, thus giving France a voting bloc somewhat similar to the British Commonwealth and continued international status as a great power. Since

1960 France has managed its relations with its former African colonies very carefully. The new French embassies, often located in the same buildings as the former colonial administrations, provided desperately needed financial, technical and military assistance to the new nations, thus ensuring their continued dependence on France. National currencies were pegged to the French franc, effectively linking their economies to that of France. Military agreements allowed the French to station their own troops in each nation, and gave them widespread powers over national armies. The French military has intervened in the former African colonies over twenty times since independence, not including the frequent involvement of private French mercenaries in conflicts there. Even without the benefit of arms, France has frequently bribed or intimidated Francophone African officials into accepting its proposals. As a result, at times African independence has seemed more illusory than real.

Finally, culture has continued to be an important part of France's influence over its former colonies. Even though the days of the 'civilising mission' are long gone, still France devotes significant resources to the maintenance of French culture overseas. The fact that 100 million people in the world speak French as their primary language has been a cornerstone of such efforts, and the French government channels aid to the former empire to ensure that the language is taught and supported with educational materials. Out of this concern for French as a global language has developed the Francophone movement, which links French-speaking countries throughout the world in a series of meetings and cultural exchanges. The first Francophone summit brought representatives of forty governments to Paris in 1986. Many members of elite social and political groups from the old colonies also continue to attend French universities, thereby helping to transmit the values of French learning and civilization back to their own countries.

But the relationships between France and the former colonies have not been one-way since 1960. Since the late 1960s the majority of immigrants to France have come from the old empire, making a significant contribution to the national economy and often posing troubling questions about the future character of French society and culture. Many French people now travel to Francophone areas as tourists, not colonial officials or settlers; it is perhaps no accident that Club Med was beginning to create a network of tropical vacation villages just as France was losing its formal empire. Books and movies about France's heritage of empire have become very popular in the late twentieth century, and novels by Francophone writers like Tahar ben Jalloun and Patrick Chamoiseau have won the nation's highest literary honours. 'World beat' music from Africa and North Africa is not only widely followed but has in a sense become French, as have culinary imports like North African cous-cous. The formal French empire may be no more, but its traces in French culture and life are still very much visible today.

At no time in France's modern history has its empire played such an important role in national affairs as the middle of the twentieth century, from the defeat of 1940 to the end of the Algerian war in 1962. The paradox that opened this chapter could not be sustained indefinitely, so that the liberation of the metropole in 1944 led inexorably to the liberation of the colonies over the next two decades. As Frantz Fanon, the black French writer from Martinique, pointed out in *The Wretched of the Earth*, colonialism was the Third World equivalent of fascism in Europe. One could not logically oppose one without condemning the other. The tragedy of postwar decolonisation arose from the difficulty so many French people, including some who had been active in the Resistance, found in learning that basic lesson. Ultimately, de Gaulle and others realised that France could only hope to retain influence over colonised peoples if it granted their desires for independence. Although France kept a great deal of power over its former colonies, especially in Africa, accepting their independence was no meaningless gesture. Instead, it constituted a fundamental recognition that the universalist value of liberty so dear to the French had, if it was to have any meaning, to be applied universally, even in cases where the liberation desired was liberation from the French themselves.

In France, writers and other creative individuals had taken the lead in the debates over decolonisation, and more broadly over the lessons of the Second World War for questions of human freedom in France and throughout the world. They more than any other group saw the links between anti-fascism and anti-colonialism. Yet the French intelligentsia was by no means monolithic in the postwar period, nor did it exercise a monopoly on French culture in general. The next chapter will deal with France's intellectuals in the postwar years, showing how their own perspectives on the legacy of the Resistance evolved and changed to meet the challenges of the late twentieth century.

CHAPTER FIVE

FRENCH CULTURE AND THE INTELLIGENTSIA

Few phenomena typify French culture to a greater extent than the intellectual, or are seen as more classically 'French'. Let us start with a caricature. The French intellectual is a man (usually) who lives in Paris (almost always), especially in the Latin Quarter, Saint-Germain-des-Prés, or other Left Bank neighbourhoods. He is usually to be found sitting at café tables, drinking glasses of red wine or cups of strong espresso and chain-smoking French cigarettes. Thus fortified, he spends his time endlessly discussing abstract philosophy or other types of learned knowledge, and making pronouncements about politics, morality and the general state of the world. When not so occupied he can be found teaching university classes, attending conferences on scholarly questions with other intellectuals, or organising political rallies. Most of all, he is a man who writes: newspaper editorials, academic articles, political manifestoes, collections of essays, and various types of fiction, works whose high quality is often equalled by their social impact.

Like most caricatures, this one presents in exaggerated form certain essential characteristics. Intellectuals have traditionally played an important role in French public life, far more so than in Britain or the United States. In France, the intellectual is generally defined as an individual engaged in creative pursuits in the arts and sciences who uses those insights to intervene in broader political and social questions. The intellectual's role as creator and disseminator of culture, especially French culture, gives her or him the right (indeed the responsibility) to voice opinions about public affairs and challenge erroneous or malevolent policies. This conception of the intellectual as social critic is far removed from both the idea of the ivory tower academic and the politician interested in nothing but power and votes. In France, politicians have traditionally been expected to display not just interest in but mastery of French culture, and even professors interested in the most obscure topics are granted the privilege of speaking out on issues of broader concern.

Intellectuals played an especially important role in French public life in the two decades after the Liberation. The above characterisation is drawn from stereotypes that took form during those years; indeed, some would view it as the portrait of one famous intellectual in particular, Jean-Paul Sartre. The Second World War and the Occupation had both traumatised and transformed France's intelligentsia, giving it a cohesion and singleness of purpose striking in their intensity. Probably no other group in French society so heartily embraced anti-fascism and the spirit of the Resistance, or did more to keep it alive long after 1944. More than before the war, the belief in political activism, or *engagement*, became central to what it meant to be a French intellectual, and the politics were almost always those of the Left. The great student and worker uprising of May 1968 testified dramatically to the significance of ideas and intellectuals in French politics. Moreover, theoretical and academic discussion and writing became a major French cultural export in the postwar years. Paris achieved new prominence as an (and in some ways *the*) intellectual centre of the postwar world, and academic polemics originating on the Left Bank were followed avidly by writers, professors and students from Argentina to Yugoslavia.

May 1968 also serves as an important demarcation in postwar French intellectual life. The fading of the dream of romantic revolution brought about an important political shift among the intelligentsia, a move to the Right all the more striking given its abrupt character and the traditional progressive colouration of academic ideologies in France. This political sea-change went along with a decline in the cohesion of the intellectual community, so that France's writers and thinkers no longer spoke with one voice, and consequently exercised less of an impact on the nation's public affairs. Finally, what it actually meant to be an intellectual changed, in response to broader changes in French popular culture. The evolution of French intellectuals from postwar solidarity to post-1968 malaise is, therefore, an especially revealing example of France's transformation during the last half of the twentieth century.

FROM EXISTENTIALISM TO STRUCTURALISM

Like everyone else in France, intellectuals were shocked by the defeat of 1940, by its sudden and cataclysmic nature. As the initial shock wore off, however, feelings of hopelessness gave way to a determination to take action. Even more so than the Resistance in general, intellectuals who took up the anti-fascist cause did so out of a desire not only to rescue France from the Nazis, but also to correct the inequities and confusion of the interwar years. The nation's creative genius would purify the nation, leading it out of the abyss of collapse and collaboration into a bright new future. The Resistance thus offered French intellectuals a chance to assume a new level of national leadership, and as a result no social group in France was more prominently represented in its ranks. These ranged from Marc

Bloch, the eminent historian whose moving *Strange Defeat* summed up the tragedy of 1940, to Paul Langevin, physicist at the Sorbonne, to a group of anthropologists at Paris' Musée de l'Homme who formed one of the first Resistance networks in the city. The main contribution of these intellectuals was writing clandestine pamphlets, articles, newspapers and books all condemning the Occupation and its Vichy collaborators, and calling upon the people of France to fight for a new day. One of the most effective Resistance statements was the classically simple poem 'Liberté', by Paul Eluard, a cry for freedom disguised as an innocent love poem.

The experience of the Resistance also created a new relationship between French intellectuals and the Communist Party. Interactions between the two had never been easy: while some writers and thinkers had admired the PCF's commitment to social justice and revolution, they had generally rejected its authoritarianism and attempts to dictate political positions to them. The party had some success recruiting intellectuals during the Popular Front years, but the Nazi–Soviet Pact of 1939 had repelled many more. After 1941, however, the PCF once again took up the anti-fascist struggle, soon becoming the most radical and effective section of the national Resistance. Consequently, most intellectuals active in or sympathetic to the Resistance were willing to support the PCF as an ally, if not necessarily to join the party or agree with all its positions. Prominent intellectuals who were PCF members, like the poet Louis Aragon and writer Claude Morgan, took the lead in crafting alliances between the two groups. Aside from their efforts, the PCF appealed to many not only because of its heroism in the anti-Nazi struggle and its progressive positions, but also because its working-class base offered intellectuals a chance to connect with the masses who never read philosophy or wrote poetry. Writers and other creative spirits flocked to the National Writers' Committee, created by the PCF to bring together anti-fascist intellectuals, which became the most successful of all the wartime 'front' groups organised by the party.

The victory over fascism gave France's intellectuals an unprecedented level of national influence, as a key part of the Resistance that had saved the nation's honour and won the war. Just as the Resistance in general enjoyed leadership based more on moral superiority and heroism than on majority status in France, so too could intellectuals who had taken part in the anti-Nazi struggle claim the right to direct the affairs of the nation because of their expertise and dedication to justice. Yet it soon became clear after the Liberation that moral standing would not alone guarantee political power, as the purer elements of the Resistance were gradually shouldered aside by more experienced career politicians. More than virtually any other group in French society, intellectuals sought to maintain the activism and commitment of the wartime years. For years after the war one's wartime record determined one's access to publishing opportunities and general reception in intellectual circles. This was especially true in Paris, far and away the dominant centre of French intellectual life, where networks and connections were everything. Immediately after the Liberation a debate raged on the Left Bank about how to treat those intellectuals who had collaborated, with the great majority insisting on a hard line. As Paul Eluard put it in March 1945, 'No jewel is more precious/Than the desire to avenge the innocent' (Lottman, 1991: 221). During the late 1940s the Communist Party exercised an inordinate influence on the intellectual life of the Left Bank, through its control of the National Writers' Committee and several prestigious journals like *Europe* and *Esprit*. Louis Aragon, the party's most important literary figure, reigned as an unofficial cultural czar, making and breaking writers' careers at will.

Yet this continued allegiance to the ideals of the Resistance could not hide the fact that the victory over fascism had not created a perfect world, nor could it prevent the development of the Cold War. This sense of both commitment to the struggle for freedom and disillusionment with its results lies at the heart of the existentialist wave in postwar France. An abstract philosophy whose roots go back to Kierkegaard and which owed its modern character to German thinkers like Martin Heidegger and Karl Jaspers, the existentialism of Paris in the 1940s and 1950s was more a cultural phenomenon than a strict academic epistemology. Jean-Paul Sartre symbolised existentialism more than anyone else in France, and its history was intimately interwoven with his character as a thinker. The ultimate Parisian intellectual, Sartre was a Renaissance man of letters rather than a philosopher in the strict sense of the word, a man who wrote novels, philosophy, drama and essays, all very well. A relatively obscure *lycée* professor until the late 1930s, Sartre had studied German philosophy as an academic exercise. He published his first existentialist work, *Nausea*, in 1938, yet not until the war did the basic outlines of his philosophy become clear. The war and Occupation forced Sartre to confront political questions and the struggle for freedom, leading him to participate in Resistance networks in Paris. These experiences led Sartre to write what would become the Bible of the existentialist movement, *Being and Nothingness*, which he published in 1943.

The heart of the book's argument, and of existentialist philosophy in general, revolved around the tension between existence and consciousness. Existence represented everything material and earthly; it was the fate of mankind, the basis of humanity. Consciousness, in contrast, was insubstantial, 'nothingness', lighter than air. Yet it was consciousness that made man human, and that enabled man to strive for freedom. It represented humanity shaping its own destiny. This struggle was by no means an easy process, and in fact was generally doomed to failure. Yet man could not do otherwise than eternally fight to be free, thus shaping his own destiny and the world he lived in. Existentialism was thus an austere philosophy, one that viewed life as a continual and often futile struggle to transcend existence. It transformed the political activism of the Resistance into the philosophical imperative of *engagement*, arguing that only by taking a stand could man hope to be free. In the years of the Occupation and the Liberation, when those who took action risked not only great personal danger but also being practically and morally wrong, this was heady stuff indeed.

After the war existentialism soon became the dominant intellectual current on the Left Bank. In the autumn of 1945 several events came together to promote the new philosophy. In October, Sartre, his lifelong companion Simone de Beauvoir and several other prominent Parisian intellectuals published the first issue of *Les Temps Modernes*, the literary and political journal that was to become (and remains to this day) the standard bearer of the Left Bank intelligentsia. At the same time both Sartre and de Beauvoir published important novels, and Sartre delivered a major public lecture entitled 'Is Existentialism a Humanism?'. Almost overnight Sartre and his colleagues became the subjects of a media feeding frenzy, as journalists from throughout France descended upon Saint-Germain-des-Prés in search of the latest intellectual fad. Existentialism was linked with the cafés, jazz clubs and youth culture of the Left Bank, so that anyone who affected a certain world-weary air and possessed even a minimal familiarity with Sartre's writings could claim to be an existentialist. By the late 1940s existentialism had become part of the general culture of Parisian intellectuals, so much so that many leading figures, most notably the writer Albert Camus, began to deny publicly allegiance to its ideas.

Existentialism owed its success to its conformity with the mood of France in the years after the Liberation: the hope for a new world and the despair over the Cold War and the fading of the Resistance ideals, and the continued belief that intellectuals should be engaged in politics. Throughout the 1950s and 1960s, long after existentialism had ceased to be new, French intellectuals remained wedded to progressive ideas and activism. This entailed a relationship with the PCF that was often close but never straightforward. Sartre never joined the party, for example, and he and many others sharply criticised the Soviet Union's invasion of Hungary in 1956. Yet their criticisms of the United States were far sharper, and in general France's writers and thinkers kept their faith in some kind of socialist future for their nation and the world. In particular, they took the lead in linking support for the ideals of the Resistance to the struggle against imperialism. Intellectuals led the domestic opposition to the Algerian war, and by the 1960s many had become fascinated with Chinese Maoism, elevating support for Asian and African liberation movements into the ideology of *Tiers Mondisme*, or 'Third Worldism'.

Yet the *engagement* of the Left Bank intellectuals did not go un-challenged. The writer Raymond Aron, from the same intellectual generation as Sartre, rejected the left-wing tilt of many of his colleagues, championing instead the liberal values of the USA. In his 1955 book, *The Opium of the Intellectuals,* he attacked Marxism as an irrational religion and its Parisian supporters as hypocrites and intellectually backward. More significant was the challenge posed by Albert Camus, one of the leaders of the intellectual Resistance and winner of the Nobel Prize for Literature. Often linked with Sartre as an existentialist writer, in 1951 Camus published his long essay, *The Rebel*, a long, historical and philosophical treatise which contended that rebellions tended to move from their original humanism to despotism and terror. Rather than political engagement, Camus preached moderation and tolerance in public affairs. The essay caused a highly publicised breach between Camus and Sartre, one that remained unresolved at the time of Camus' death in a car crash in 1960.

Such attacks on Left Bank orthodoxy nonetheless fitted well into the overall politicised climate of postwar intellectual Paris. A more fund-amental ideological and theoretical shift arose with the development of structuralist philosophy. Originally a specific approach to linguistics, dev-eloped by the Swiss scholar Ferdinand de Saussure at the beginning of the twentieth century, by the mid-1960s structuralism was looming large as the most important successor to existentialism among French intellectuals. In a nutshell, structuralists argued that human life was conditioned and ulti-mately determined by cognitive and institutional structures, especially those based in language itself. These structures functioned not according to historical context, let alone human desire, but in relationship to their own internal make-up. The major task of scholars was to analyse and under-stand these structures, which would therefore give the most important insights into human behaviour and the human condition. Structuralism was developed by intellectuals working in several different fields. In 1958 the anthropologist Claude Lévi-Strauss published his *Structural Anthropology,* emphasising the basic structures of mythic belief systems and attacking previous anthropological approaches. This was followed by literary critic Roland Barthes' 1963 study of Racine, stressing the study of the text rather than the author, and psychologist Jacques Lacan's 1966 *Ecrits*, which argued that the unconscious was entirely dependent upon linguistic structures.

Structuralism did not completely break with the postwar traditions of the Left Bank. Many of its key figures, like Barthes, were Marxists, and shared a critical approach to contemporary society. However, whereas Sartre and his colleagues had championed the importance of individual agency, the structuralists contended that man was basically helpless before an array of structural constraints. In opposition to the traditional humanism of the existentialists, structuralism posited a universe in which man seemed to count for relatively little. For example, the *Annales* school of history, which was strongly influenced by structuralism, emphasised geographical and economic structures over historical events, so much so that at times its practitioners seemed to be writing histories in which nothing ever happened. For an historiographical tradition dominated by the story of events (in particular one event, the French Revolution) this was a major departure.

Structuralism did not develop in a vacuum, but reflected its times. It arose in part from the unprecedented expansion of the social sciences, a field traditionally weak in French universities and intellectual life. These often betrayed a strong intellectual influence from the United States, where during the 1950s and 1960s sociology and similar disciplines received not only academic prestige but significant government support. Funding from the Rockefeller and Ford foundations helped found the *Ecole des Hautes études en sciences sociales* in 1975, for example. Yet American influence was due less to direct financial support and more to the fact that French society was evolving in a direction similar to its trans-Atlantic counterpart. By the 1960s changes in the structures of France's economy and society had made major improvements in the living standards of average citizens. More significantly, good times brought a new sense of stability to the nation, one in which change seemed less important than continuity. The new emphasis on technocracy suggested that faceless bureaucrats, such as those who devised and implemented the Five Year Plans, were more significant than charismatic political leaders or other individuals. The heroic age of the Resistance, of individuals fighting for freedom was long past; moreover, by the early 1960s decolonisation, the colonial equivalent of such struggles, had come to an end. The anti-historical tendency of the structuralists developed in a climate of prosperity, success and peace, making it easy to believe the arguments of American modernisation theorists that the world was witnessing 'the end of history'. The romantic revolutionary of the existentialists must therefore give way to structuralism's Organisation Man.

In general, creative life in France accompanied structuralism in the move away from political activism and towards greater abstraction and pure intellectualism. The literary wave known as the New Novel, championed by authors like Alain Robbe-Grillet and Nathalie Sarraute, produced books that emphasised internal reflection and literary experimentation at the expense of plot, description, or social and historical context. Similarly, the New Wave filmmakers, with the singular exception of Jean-Luc Godard, avoided any kind of social commentary, generally preferring arty dramas and comedies about middle-class young Parisians like themselves. During the 1960s, therefore, intellectual and creative life seemed to retreat into itself, abandoning the claim to moral leadership of society posed by the postwar existentialism. However, many still believed in the values of the Resistance. Moreover, a new generation was arising that would pose its own challenges to French society. As the drama of May 1968 would reveal, intellectuals still had the power to shake up their nation and make arguments that would be listened to by France as a whole.

FRENCH UNIVERSITIES AND THE CRISIS OF MAY 1968

1968 was an extraordinary year not only in France but around the globe, a year marked by student uprisings in America, Japan, Mexico, and many other nations. Yet in perhaps no other country was the student movement as far-reaching and powerful as in France. Starting at a peripheral campus of the University of Paris, the movement quickly escalated into a full-blown social and political crisis that nearly overthrew the Fifth Republic. Few observers would have predicted such a massive leftist revolt in an advanced capitalist country during the late 1960s, especially one as prosperous and economically healthy. After a long hiatus, in 1968 Paris resumed its nineteenth-century role as the world capital of revolution.

The power of the May movement arose in large part from the still important role of intellectuals in French society. University students are intellectuals, of course, and the postwar expansion of higher education in France gave the nation's intelligentsia a mass base of unprecedented size. Moreover, the movement developed in large part out of critiques of French society, and of the traditional French Left, formulated by leading writers and thinkers. Student protests briefly gave these ideas, and their authors, a level of influence in national affairs unmatched since the Liberation. This activism took the existentialist ideal of *engagement* to an entirely new level. Finally, the collapse of the May movement had a tremendous impact on French intellectual life, setting the tone for debates that would occur in the last decades of the twentieth century.

The history of May 1968 must be considered in the broader context of the rise of the New Left during the mid-twentieth century. The New Left was an intellectual and political movement that criticised both American-style capitalism and Soviet authoritarian communism, calling instead for a revolutionary democratic socialism free of Stalinist repression. This perspective drew upon the traditions of anti-fascism during and after the war, reinforced by a more developed critique of both sides in the Cold War. The powerful, frequently dogmatic, role of the PCF in postwar intellectual affairs engendered a lot of resentment among individuals who nonetheless refused to surrender their belief in radical political change. In the late 1940s and 1950s a group of intellectuals led by Cornelius Castoriadis and Claude Lefort started a journal, *Socialism or Barbarism*, which harshly criticised the Soviet model, arguing it was not socialism at all, but rather bureaucratic state capitalism. A major turning point occurred in 1956, when Jean-Paul Sartre and many other Left Bank intellectuals condemned the Soviet suppression of the Hungarian uprising, portraying it as a popular socialist revolt against an authoritarian foreign power. This position posed an implicit (sometimes explicit) challenge to the French Communist Party, which some radical intellectuals viewed as not only authoritarian but also lacking in dynamism or new ideas. Such critical perspectives did not spare the other major party of the French Left, the Socialists. While the SFIO's democratic commitment was not seriously in doubt, most felt it had long ago abandoned any revolutionary mission, instead allowing itself to become a part of the capitalist system. In 1956 a group of dissidents split away from the SFIO, angered largely by its refusal to criticise the Algerian war, and went on to found the Unified Socialist Party, giving the New Left an institutional framework.

At the same time, French intellectuals began developing a new critique of capitalism, based upon an exploration of the problems of affluence. By the 1960s the argument that capitalism impoverished the working class was obviously no longer viable in a nation enjoying the greatest prosperity it had ever known. However, one could and did attack both the nature of work, and consumer culture, as oppressive. Some contended that under advanced capitalism oppression had changed, so that issues of alienation, rather than impoverishment, became key. Workers and others might have enough to eat, but nonetheless lacked any sense of control over their own lives, or ability to express their own desires and creativity. The Marxist philosopher Henri Lefebvre led a rediscovery of the writings of the younger Karl Marx, emphasising humanism and the problems of alienation. He used them to advance a theory of total revolution, economic, social, political, spiritual and sexual. His influence was greatest upon the young scholars and artists of the so-called Situationist International, who used street theatre and other performances to criticise consumer society and the *status quo*. In his 1967 book, *Society of the Spectacle*, filmmaker Guy DeBord charged postwar France with using consumerism to silence its critics and reduce its citizens to a state of passivity and helplessness. Ultimately, therefore, the New Left judged both capitalism and communism to be bureaucratic, alienating and anti-democratic.

This critique of Cold War bipolarism and the search for a revolutionary democratic alternative provided the intellectual background for the events of May 1968. However, these critiques would have remained limited to a few writers and thinkers but for the transformation of French higher education in the 1960s. By the middle of that decade many of the postwar baby boom generation had reached college age, dramatically swelling enrolments in the nation's universities. Moreover, increasing affluence and economic sophistication created a need for more and more college-educated workers. As a result, the number of French college students nearly tripled between 1958 and 1968; by 1967 enrolments were roughly ten times what they had been thirty years earlier. Universities expanded rapidly in the 1960s in order to keep pace. The University of Paris expanded beyond the old campus of the Sorbonne, creating several new branches in the city and its suburbs. Yet rapid growth was not accompanied by structural reforms, or rethinking the mission of higher education. University administrations remained rigidly centralised and conservative in their approach to education. Most professors continued to teach their classes as formal lectures, in spite of student desires for more casual and intimate intellectual interactions. A classic liberal arts curriculum dominated, not taking into account student needs for job preparation or requests for classes more relevant to the contemporary world. In addition, universities were often overcrowded and a nightmare of bureaucratic rules and regulations. The fact that by the late 1960s less than half of new university students eventually graduated underlined the malaise of French higher education.

When the trouble started, it did so at a campus that exemplified the crisis of the postwar French university. The branch of the University of Paris in the suburb of Nanterre had been founded in 1964, and grew rapidly from 4,000 to 15,000 students in three years. Its location stood in sharp contrast to that of the Sorbonne, sitting in the traditional heart of French student culture, the Latin Quarter. Whereas the Quarter offered a wide range of bookstores, cafés, restaurants, nightclubs and other diversions, Nanterre arose in the middle of empty fields, a campus made of the same kinds of soulless high-rise building erected by public housing authorities all over the postwar Paris suburbs. At the same time, the Nanterre students generally came from affluent backgrounds, and most specialised in the arts and social sciences, intellectual disciplines most likely to offer critiques of the *status quo*. Like French students elsewhere, they had to deal with overcrowded classrooms and inadequate housing space, and chafed under infantilising restrictions like a ban on visitors of the opposite sex in their dorm rooms.

Such conditions provided fertile soil for student activists. In late 1967 sociology students and some others created a group called the *enragés*, which soon took over the main student organisation at Nanterre and staked out a political position on the militant Left. Not only did it develop a critique of the modern university as more dedicated to the maintenance of capitalism than to education and scholarship, but also challenged establishment policies on national and international issues. Whereas the Socialist and Communists criticised America's war in Vietnam by calling for peace in that country, Nanterre's *enragés* went further, supporting an outright victory for the Viet Cong. Like student activists elsewhere in Europe, especially West Germany and Italy, Nanterre's activists embraced the New

Left and struggles for Third World Liberation. With heroes as diverse as Mao Zedong, Malcolm X and Che Guevara, they demanded an alternative to the traditional French Left. In January 1968, after returning from an international student conference in Berlin, the *enragés* staged a major demonstration against the Vietnam War at Nanterre. This triggered a series of protest actions which soon threw the suburban campus into turmoil. Attempts by the university administration to isolate the leaders and stop the movement only led to charges of repression and the radicalisation of many more students. Leaders like Daniel Cohn-Bendit and Alain Krivine emerged to lead the struggle, trying to coordinate a wide range of student activist organisations. In March Cohn-Bendit, Krivine and others occupied the main administration building on campus, while other Nanterre students staged attacks in Paris on symbols of US imperialism like the Bank of America and American Express. Confronted with this escalating uproar, university officials responded by closing the Nanterre campus at the beginning of May, hoping that militant ardour would cool over the summer months.

This was a strategic mistake, for rather than simply going home and forgetting about the movement, the Nanterre *enragés* transferred the struggle to the Sorbonne. The struggle thus moved from the isolation of a suburban campus to the heart of French intellectual and academic life. On 2 May the Nanterre activists occupied the central courtyard of the Sorbonne, leading administrators there to call in the police the next day. Many students who were not activists nonetheless resented the intrusion of armed police into the university and came out in support of the activists, as did many high school students and university lecturers. Violence erupted between students and police, setting off a series of demonstrations over the next week that climaxed with the erection of barricades in the Latin Quarter on the night of 10–11 May, the first time Paris had seen barricades since the Liberation. The fighting was so intense that people on the metro under the area that night began crying as tear gas wafted down through ventilation ducts from the embattled streets above. At this point the government responded to charges of police brutality by reopening the Sorbonne, which promptly became a non-stop debating society on how to make the revolution. The trade unions declared a one-day protest strike and 800,000 supporters of the movement marched through Paris shouting 'de Gaulle! Ten years, that's enough!'

Had the May movement ended at this point it would have been an important student victory, similar to many others around the world in 1968. Instead, it soon turned into a national crisis. The student leaders viewed their movement as a challenge to capitalist society in general, not just the universities, and tried to enlist working-class support for their cause. On 13 May, for example, a delegation marched from the Latin

Quarter to the giant Renault factory outside Paris and called upon the auto workers there to join the struggle. Although union leaders, especially those of the Communist CGT, rejected such pleas, many workers heard them, and soon a series of spontaneous strikes began throughout French industry. Many of the strikers were relatively well paid and had secure jobs, yet resented the pressures to increase production rates and the absence of any workplace democracy or sense of control over one's labour. Often the strikers occupied their factories, demanding a greater say in how they were run. The strike wave began in the provinces, in the aircraft and other branches of heavy industry, then spread throughout the economy. Not only blue-collar workers but also many professionals in the nation's cultural sector took part. Employees at ORTF, the national radio and television office, went on strike in protest against the lack of autonomy in the media. Turmoil in the film industry forced the cancellation of the Cannes film festival. Even the nation's football players joined the movement, occupying the offices of the National Football Federation and proclaiming '*le football aux footballeurs*'. By the third week of May 10 million French men and women had gone on strike, almost always against the advice of the unions or the traditional Left parties, and France seemed poised on the brink of revolution.

Only at this point did the administration of Charles de Gaulle realise the gravity of the situation. De Gaulle himself had not taken the student movement very seriously, at one point suggesting that students were agitating for the right to have mistresses in their dorm rooms. Indeed, after the fighting in the Latin Quarter ended he felt so secure about domestic affairs that he left for a state visit to Romania. On 18 May the wave of strikes forced de Gaulle to cut short his diplomatic trip and return to Paris. There he found a nation that seemed to have dissolved into an anarchist carnival. There was a surreal spirit of joy, even of celebration about the May strikes, a sense of liberation from the ennui of everyday life. Student leaders at the Sorbonne welcomed anyone and everyone to come and speak his or her mind about any social issue, while nearby the students at the School of Fine Arts were busily turning out revolutionary posters with romantic slogans like 'Be a realist! Demand the impossible!' Some occupied factories created workers' councils that began planning for a more demo-cratic workplace, while in the countryside there were stories of farmers defiantly blocking highways with their prized tractors. Faced with such turmoil de Gaulle immediately took action. He announced reforms of higher education, and his prime minister, Georges Pompidou, began negotiations with union leaders over ending the strikes. The latter produced the Grenelle Accords, which granted significant wage increases and more vacation time. Yet the crisis continued, and some union leaders were booed by striking workers when they presented the Grenelle concessions. By the end of May many, if not most, people in France had concluded that de Gaulle was finished, and the end of his government only a matter of time.

Then on 29 May Charles de Gaulle simply disappeared. For the head of state to leave the country without telling anyone is of course highly unusual, and in such turbulent times even suggested the possibility that the revolution had triumphed. Yet de Gaulle did not go far. He flew off to Baden-Baden, headquarters of the French military forces in West Germany, and there met with General Massu. It is not known what the two men said to each other, but de Gaulle returned to Paris that evening with a new determination to end the crisis. He went on television that night to make a forceful speech promising reform but also demanding order and a return to normality. Warning against the dangers of a Communist seizure of power, de Gaulle announced he would not resign, instead dissolving the National Assembly and scheduling new elections for June. This time de Gaulle's appeal fell upon receptive ears. While many French people were obviously dissatisfied with the normal order of things, they did not want a Communist revolution. Moreover, by this time ordinary citizens were simply getting tired of disorder, of long lines at gas stations and mountains of uncollected trash. 500,000 Gaullist supporters staged an impromptu march down the Champs Elysées, loudly backing de Gaulle's appeal. Over the next few weeks the strike wave fizzled out as strikers began drifting back to work, leaving the student activists more and more isolated. When elections were held at the end of June the Gaullists scored a crushing victory, in large part because the organised Left had failed to offer something new. Charles de Gaulle thus emerged triumphant, and the great near-revolution of May 1968 soon seemed like only a distant memory.

FROM *ENGAGEMENT* TO NEO-CONSERVATISM

Although students and other young people clearly led the May movement, many established intellectuals also took part. For the most part, they supported the cause of the *enragés*. Not all were as enthusiastic as the Belgian Marxist economist Ernest Mandel, who joyfully applauded the revolutionary spirit of the barricade builders in the Latin Quarter (even though he was unknowingly watching his own car burn). A few, notably Raymond Aron, condemned the student revolutionaries as irresponsible anarchists. Yet many more marched alongside the student activists, helped hand out leaflets, and called upon French authorities to listen to the voice of youth. More generally, May 1968 represented the high point of public activism by intellectuals in the postwar era. At no other time in the postwar era did their ideas carry such weight in public events. The May events became the signal experience of the New Left in France, and those who believed in revolutionary democracy and a third way between capitalism and Communism carefully guarded its memory. At the same time, the sudden collapse of the movement caused consternation among many French writers and thinkers, gradually bringing about a major re-evaluation of ideas about politics, liberation and the public responsibility of intellectuals. The most important trend among French intellectuals after 1968 was a massive shift to the political Right, and reassessments of the May movement played a key role in that shift. In particular, some young intellectuals who had actively supported the movement began to question the experience by the late 1970s, in the process setting the tone for intellectual debate in France as the twentieth century approached its end.

Perhaps the most significant intellectual trend of the late twentieth century in France was the evolution of structuralism into what became known as post-structuralism, or post-modernism. This trend had begun well before the events of May 1968, but they gave it a new impetus and significance. The magnitude of the near revolution challenged structuralism by showing that individualism and spontaneity still had a role to play in human affairs, yet its ultimate failure also suggested that structural analyses retained their importance. The leading exponent of the new post-structuralism was the philosopher Michel Foucault. Whereas Foucault's early works had emphasised linguistic structures as the key to human understanding, by the 1970s he began to distance himself from structuralism and devote more attention to questions of power and marginality in society and culture. Politically on the Left, Foucault became director of the Department of Philosophy at the University of Paris-Vincennes, a campus created after 1968 with a strong New Left orientation. In books like *Discipline and Punish* and *The History of Sexuality*, he considered the ways in which modern societies constituted themselves by excluding undesirable groups and ideas. Rejecting traditional history as the linear narrative of the victors, instead Foucault practised what he called the 'genealogy' of societies. Rejecting Marxism's emphasis on class struggle and historical evolution, Foucault focused upon marginal groups like prisoners and homosexuals. Like the young *enragés* of May 1968 he saw revolution as encompassing all aspects of human existence. To a much greater extent, however, he began to question the idea of revolution in general, at least revolution conceived as a single cataclysmic event. Since power was endlessly complex and diffused throughout human societies, true change could only occur on an infinite number of interrelated levels.

Foucault's philosophy and the tenets of post-structuralism had a major impact not only in France but throughout the intellectual world. By the early 1980s scholars at universities throughout the Western world and beyond were reading Foucault and debating his ideas. Foucault himself became the kind of international academic superstar not seen since the heyday of Jean-Paul Sartre. Another major contributor to post-structuralism was the philosopher Jacques Derrida. In books like *On Grammatology* and *Writing and Difference*, Derrida developed his theory and method of deconstruction, arguing that the prime task of philosophers was to reveal the silences and gaps in a given text as a way of understanding the values of the societies that created them. Structures themselves therefore became the object of analysis, opening the way to an infinite fragmentation of perspectives on human existence. Just as the New Left had rejected the bipolar certainties of Cold War politics, therefore, so too did post-structuralism emphasise the complex, interconnected nature of not only power but human knowledge in general.

In the aftermath of May 1968, intellectual post-structuralism could be read either as reaffirming the idea of revolution at its most radical, or in contrast suggesting that precisely because it was so complex it was destined to remain an impossible ideal. During the 1970s the latter interpretation gradually gained the upper hand, as the memory of the May events faded and France suddenly went from prosperity to recession. The disdain expressed by the student activists of 1968 for the PCF soon became for many intellectuals a rejection of all Marxist politics. In 1974 Alexander Solzhenitsyn's *Gulag Archipelago* appeared in French translation, laying bare the horrors of Stalinist repression in the Soviet Union. This was not the first time French intellectuals had been exposed to the evils of the Soviet system, yet the increasing disenchantment with the Left gave this perspective far more influence than in earlier decades. Just how much was demonstrated by the appearance of the group known as the New Philosophers in the late 1970s. A disparate group led by the writers Andre Glucksmann and Bernard-Henri Lévy, they were young intellectuals who had been active in the May 1968 revolt, but had now concluded that Marxism and revolutionary ideology in general led not to human liberation but inevitably to totalitarianism and genocide instead. In 1977 Lévy published *Barbarism with a Human Face*, which argued that the crimes of Stalinism were inherent in socialism itself. Again, there was little here that one could not have found in the writings of Camus or Aron a generation earlier, but the increasingly conservative political and intellectual climate of the 1970s made media stars of the New Philosophers.

A more fundamental challenge to the intellectual Left came from the ranks of revisionist historians. Communism and the Russian Revolution had been so attractive precisely because they seemed to further the tradition of the French Revolution, more than any other single event the basis of French national identity. Yet in the late 1970s a new group of historians, led by François Furet, challenged the positive image of the Revolution. In his 1978 *Interpreting the French Revolution*, Furet argued that the Revolution had begun well by overthrowing royal despotism and establishing liberal rights, but then had deviated into a totalitarian phase of Jacobin dictatorship and Terror. This not only represented a fundamental attack on the dominant Marxist historiography of the French Revolution, but also strongly implied that revolution in general was destructive. In particular, Furet's approach rejected the idea that one could justify Communist violence with the example of Jacobinism, precisely by condemning the Terror itself. This perspective soon became the dominant interpretation of the French Revolution not only in France but abroad as well. In the 1983 film *Danton*, for example, Robespierre was represented as a crypto-Bolshevik, whereas Danton appeared as the champion of liberal humanism.

By the early 1980s France's intellectuals had massively embraced anti-Communism. During that decade they fervently supported the gathering popular resistance to the Soviet regimes in Eastern Europe, especially Poland, and loudly cheered the collapse of the Berlin Wall and the Soviet Union. The old alliance with the PCF was conclusively broken, so much so that one route to intellectual celebrity on the Left Bank had become joining the PCF, quitting or getting oneself expelled, and then writing a book lambasting the party. In this new atmosphere, the old postwar days of political *engagement* seemed very far away. Moreover, the nature of intellectual life had shifted in other ways as well. Traditional exponents of the written word, by the end of the twentieth century French intellectuals had learned to embrace the electronic media. Indeed, part of the success of New Philosophers like Glucksmann and Lévy was their good looks and ease with television. From 1975 to 1990 the main venue for writers hoping to make a name for themselves was not *Les Temps Modernes* or any other Parisian journal, but rather *Apostrophes*, a widely-followed weekly television show devoted to reviewing popular and important books. Media *savoir-faire* had become very important to Paris's leading intellectuals, so much so that the flamboyant writer Jean-Edern Hallier was widely suspected of having staged his own kidnapping in the early 1980s.

Such changes have led many commentators to speak of the decline of the traditional French intellectual and the end of the Left Bank mandarins. Certainly, although literary and philosophical trends have come and gone, there has been no major conceptual breakthrough since the advent of post-structuralism. Moreover, decentralisation and the growth of new provincial universities have to a certain extent loosened the iron grip of Paris on the nation's writers and thinkers. Yet in many respects the French intellectual remains a special breed. The character of their political convictions may have changed, yet intellectuals continue to believe in the importance of political commitment, and also tend to speak as a cohesive group, in spite of many internal disputes. They remain committed to writing for a broader public, in contrast to the ivory tower isolation of most academics in Britain and America. Although the democratisation of higher education in France has reduced the prestige of writers and philosophers, at the same time it has vastly increased the market for their ideas. Not only do radio and television shows like *Apostrophes* reach millions, but one can find learned texts prominently displayed for sale in ordinary department stores throughout the nation. Berets and dim Left Bank cafés may give way to televised media events and personal web sites, but the underlying commitment of French intellectuals to the world of ideas and to public debate will undoubtedly endure well into the future.

The shift of intellectual gravity in France from Left to Right illustrated the decline of the spirit of the Resistance and other postwar concerns as France entered the last quarter of the twentieth century. It spoke to the changing nature of French life in an era of dissolving certainties and new challenges. The ways in which the French confronted the birth of this new era will constitute the subject of the final chapter of this book.

CHAPTER SIX

FRANCE IN THE MITTERRAND ERA

On 8 January 1996, almost exactly a half-century after Charles de Gaulle angrily walked off the French political scene, former French president François Mitterrand died at the age of seventy-nine. No man had done more to shape the destiny of France in the last quarter of the twentieth century, and only de Gaulle himself equalled the importance of his impact on French life since the Second World War. Leader of the French Socialist Party since 1971, in 1981 he was elected the first Socialist president of France under the Fifth Republic. He served in that office for fourteen years, making him the longest-lived French head of state since Emperor Napoleon III in the nineteenth century. For this reason alone, no name better suits this most recent period of French history than the era of Mitterrand.

Yet more than simple longevity explains the central role played by François Mitterrand and his Socialist administration in the life of France on the eve of the millennium. One theme of this study has been the importance of the French Resistance's legacy for the history of postwar France. The nation's two most important political forces, the Gaullists and the Communists, in different ways both owed their significance after 1945 to their struggle against Nazism and Vichy. The Fourth Republic's failed attempt to prevent both from coming to power led to its political demise. At the same time, the creation of far-reaching welfare state policies, and in a broader sense postwar prosperity and the social changes it wrought among the French people, represented the achievement of an important part of the Resistance agenda. In foreign affairs, France's inability to forge a third way between the United States and the Soviet Union symbolised the limits of Resistance ideology, whereas the bitter struggles over decolonisation showed how tragedy could result when France refused to accept the adoption of that ideology by its colonial subjects.

In several ways the 'Rose Revolution' which brought Mitterrand and the Socialists to power in 1981 represented a significant departure from such preoccupations. The 1981 elections gave the Socialists an electoral majority for the first time in the party's history, and gave them greater

Plate 1 Charles de Gaulle marching down the Champs Elysées during the liberation of Paris, 25 August 1944. (Courtesy of the Agence Roger Viollet.)

Plate 2 Alternative urban transportation during the Paris transport strike, October 1947. (Courtesy of the Agence Roger Viollet.)

Plate 3 French paratroopers holding a photograph of de Gaulle during the crisis of May 1958 in Algiers. (Courtesy of the Agence Roger Viollet.)

Plate 4 Algerian women and children during the demonstration of 17 October 1961 in Paris. (Courtesy of the Agence Roger Viollet.)

Plate 5   Tear gas and street fighting in Paris, 6 May 1968.
(Courtesy of the Agence Roger Viollet.)

Plate 6   John-Paul Sartre (1905–80). (Courtesy of the Agence Roger Viollet.)

Plate 7   Ho Chi Minh (1890–1969). (Courtesy of the Agence Roger Viollet.)

Plate 8 McDonald's in Paris. (Courtesy of Earl and Donna Evleth.)

Plate 10 Suburban housing projects in Sarcelles. (Courtesy of Earl and Donna Evleth.)

Plate 9 The Montparnasse Tower in Paris. (Courtesy of Earl and Donna Evleth.)

strength than the Communists for the first time since 1945. 1981 also represented the return of the PCF to the government since its ousting in 1947. The Gaullist dominance and Communist isolation so characteristic of much of the postwar period thus came to an end. Moreover, the Mitterrand administration found itself forced to deal with economic decline as the fundamental reality of life in contemporary France. It not only had to contend with, but itself began to undertake, challenges to the welfare state, that proud creation of the postwar years. Broader social changes also indicated a transition to a new era in France. The heralded baby boom of the 1940s and 1950s came to an end, leading to new fears of an aging population. In addition, the postwar trauma of decolonisation mutated into new debates about immigration, citizenship and race, as many former colonial subjects settled in metropolitan France. Finally, the end of the Cold War and the collapse of Soviet Communism, plus the acceleration of European unification at the end of the century, sharply underscored the shifting nature of France's relationship to the rest of the world.

It is tempting to read the recent history of France as the decline of the nation's unique political and social character in favour of integration into broader international patterns. Some have chosen to regard the Mitterrand administration, for example, as representing at long last the creation of a successful centrist faction in French politics, overcoming traditional divisions between Left and Right. Such conclusions have some merit, but should also be taken with a pinch of salt. In an era of increasing multiculturalism and European integration France has retained its own traditions and singular national profile. It is noteworthy that the French chose to elect and re-elect a Socialist president during the conservative era of Reagan, Thatcher and Kohl. The last quarter of the twentieth century has brought many profound changes to French life, but any conclusions about the end of a distinctive French identity remain decidedly premature.

FROM ECONOMIC BOOM TO ECONOMIC STAGNATION

In April 1969, less than a year after his triumph over the young rebels of the May movement, Charles de Gaulle resigned the presidency and left French public life for ever. Faced with the voters' stinging rejection of his proposed referendum on decentralisation, he chose to relinquish the leadership of a nation which no longer supported his ideas and retreat into private life. Unlike after 1946, however, there would be no triumphant political comeback. In November 1970 de Gaulle died at the age of seventy-nine, bringing to a close an era which had begun with his call for resistance thirty years earlier. He was succeeded as president by his able but colourless prime minister, Georges Pompidou. Pompidou was a capable administrator and also had the good fortune to govern France during the last years of the economic boom, a period when real wages continued to rise and France overtook Britain as an economic power. His administration was a period of major construction projects, including the Montparnasse tower and the Pompidou art centre in Paris, that reflected the prosperity and optimism of those years. Yet Pompidou was also an elderly man who lacked the ability to inspire the French people, and his death in April 1974 seemed the natural end to a lackluster regime. Valéry Giscard-d'Estaing, of the Centre-Right French Democratic Union (UDF) became the new president, heading an administration dedicated both to continuing the technocratic and economic success of the Gaullists and to implementing some liberal reforms to address the grievances of the May movement.

In 1974 economic disaster struck. The central defining aspect of French life from the Liberation until the mid-1970s was a strong and growing economy. Short-term economic crises did occur, but in general growth constituted the norm, something that average citizens and national leaders could take as a given. As we have seen earlier in this book, the scope and consistency of this economic boom created a new France, one that would not have been recognisable a generation earlier. These good times came to a crashing halt by the mid-1970s, however, giving way to a persistent era of economic stagnation and decline. Unemployment, virtually unknown in France during the 1950s and 1960s, became once again a central pre-occupation for many people, especially youth. At the same time inflation rates accelerated, biting deep into the income of the average French man and woman. The political malaise that some observers had pointed to in the aftermath of May 1968 was now reinforced by a much more profound sense of unease about the quality of life and the future of the nation. Optimism turned to pessimism as France entered an uncertain new era.

The recession of the 1970s and 1980s was of course not limited to France but global in scope. The most immediate cause was the sharp hikes in the price of oil. In December 1973, OPEC, the cartel of oil-producing countries, initiated a series of major raises in the price of crude petroleum, quadrupling its value by the end of 1975. Much of the postwar economic boom, especially in the automobile industry, had relied upon cheap petroleum, so these increases sent shock waves throughout the industrialised world. The price hikes hit France, which imported 75 per cent of its oil, particularly hard, sending inflation rates up to 14 per cent. A second series of oil price increases in 1979–81 reinforced the harm done by the first, triggering spiralling rates of both inflation and unemployment throughout Europe and America.

As bad as they were, however, the oil price increases do not alone account for the severity of the economic crisis, which also reflected broader transformations in the international economy. Postwar expansion was built around American dominance of European economies, so much so that under the system created by the Bretton Woods agreements in 1944 the currencies of Western European nations were officially pegged to the dollar. This worked fine for everyone as long as the US economy remained healthy, but by the early 1970s that was no longer the case. America's pursuit of both guns and butter during the 1960s, its investment in extensive social welfare programmes at the same time as it waged a major war in Vietnam, placed a serious strain upon the national economy. More generally, the Bretton Woods system developed at a time when a wealthy and productive United States was surrounded by weak European economies struggling to recover from the devastation of the war. As Europe revived and its industries began to compete effectively with American goods, however, what had been basically a colonial structure predicated upon inequality lost some of its stability. As a result of these stresses, in August 1971 the United States abandoned the Bretton Woods system of fixed currency rates, throwing international money markets into chaos. Bereft of its central structural underpinnings, the international economy thus proved especially vulnerable to the oil price shocks of the 1970s.

The global recession also revealed and exacerbated problems within the French economy. For all the modernisation achieved in the postwar era, France still contained a sizeable sector of relatively inefficient small factories and businesses, whose limited scope became all the more significant as the nation became much more involved in the international economy during the 1960s. For example, the tiny town of Thiers in central France gloried in its artisanal cutlery industry, based on traditions going back to the thirteenth century. The cutlers of Thiers produced wonderful knives, but they were expensive and could not really compete with mass-produced products. By the 1980s the Thiers cutlery industry had largely died out, its workshops replaced by more modern factories elsewhere. France was also a nation of high labour costs, especially after the Grenelle Accords of 1968. Lack of productivity due to low levels of mechanisation and technological investment in certain sectors of the economy exacerbated the problem. The uneasy balance between the traditional and modern parts of the economy also contributed to inflation. Rising prices and currency instability had in fact been a problem for much of the postwar period, reigned in by adroit financial management and periodic adjustments like the devaluation of 1959. As the consumption levels of French men and women grew, so did the nation's balance of payments deficit. Finally, some of the most dynamic companies had shown a tendency to expand too fast, leaving them overextended and vulnerable. During an era of continuous economic growth none of these problems was insuperable, but once that growth disappeared they combined to push France deeper into recession.

After 1974, therefore, the nation saw a return to the kind of hard times it had not known since the 1930s, and that much of its population had never experienced at all. Annual growth rates, which had averaged nearly 6 per cent during the 1960s, declined to less than 3 per cent during the 1970s. Inflation rates settled at about 11 per cent per year during the 1970s, shooting up to 14 per cent during the oil crises of 1973–74 and 1979–81. Most disturbing of all was the precipitous increase in unemployment. During most of the *trentes glorieuses* France had enjoyed close to full employment, having in fact to resort to extensive immigration to staff its industries and businesses. By 1975, however, the nation had one million unemployed workers. Worse still, the unemployment rate continued to worsen during most of the rest of the century, in spite of economic upsurges that at times relieved the worst effects of the recession. From a figure of 4.0 per cent in 1975, it increased to 10.2 per cent in 1985 and 11.9 per cent in 1993, representing in that latter year 3.4 million people out of a job (Gildea, 1996).

The impact of unemployment and economic crises was felt widely but not evenly throughout the French population. Most heavily affected were industrial workers and farmers. As basic industrial production, such as coal and steel, began to shift from the developed to the Third World in general, France experienced the same crises of de-industrialisation afflicting other parts of Europe and the United States. Certain regions, such as the coal mining areas of the Nord and the steel factories of Lorraine, were particularly hard hit. In 1978, for example, the French government announced plans to close several obsolete steel mills in Lorraine, throwing 16,000 employees out of work. The news sparked a near-insurrection in the town of Longwy, prompting fears of a new May 1968. De-industrialisation was the most dramatic example of the long-term decline of the French working class in the late twentieth century. Whereas industry accounted for 39 per cent of the working population in 1975, it had diminished to 29 per cent by 1992. A similar process reshaped the nation's agricultural population. By the 1970s, thanks to its efforts to preserve some rural population in an increasingly urbanised Europe, the European Economic Community (EEC) had accumulated huge surpluses of agricultural products. It responded with plans to reduce the number of EEC farmers, favouring the larger, more modernised farms at the expense of the smaller and less productive ones. France, the biggest agricultural producer in the EEC, bore the brunt of this new policy. Those French farmers who had adapted to modern marketing and technology generally survived, but many others did not. France lost 600,000 farmers between 1975 and 1990, a major blow to the self-image of a nation whose soul had always been closely tied up with the land.

Poverty, which the victors of the Second World War had hoped would vanish under the new society, returned as a central issue for the French people. It had never entirely disappeared, even during the most prosperous times, but had been largely relegated to the margins of the society, especially immigrants and the elderly. After the mid-1970s many people who had become accustomed to secure livelihoods and all the pleasures that consumer society could provide suddenly found themselves out of a job and living from hand to mouth. Unemployment rates were highest for young people, often making it difficult for them to find decent jobs and start their own lives after school. In sharp contrast to the years of postwar prosperity, when the nation treasured and invested heavily in its youth, now young people seemed a burden and expendable. It is true that as bad as things got during the 1970s and 1980s, conditions remained far better than they had been before the Second World War. Unemployment insurance and a variety of other social benefits cushioned the impact of hard times. For example, inflation and unemployment could co-exist partly because even the unemployed continued to have a certain amount of buying power. Yet the impact of the recession was not just economic but psychological, intensifying the national dissatisfaction so evident during the crisis of May 1968.

The French government was slow to react to the problem. Georges Pompidou was dying when the oil price crisis first broke in December 1973, and the new government of Valéry Giscard-d'Estaing did not take power until the end of May 1974, by which time the economy had already taken a definite turn for the worse. Giscard-d'Estaing had previously served as the French minister of finance in the early 1960s, and his administration soon gave the task of reviving the economy top priority. Given the global nature of the recession, this was much easier said than done. Giscard-d'Estaing appointed as his prime minister Raymond Barre, one of France's leading economists. Barre's strategy for restoring economic health to the nation was deflation, cutting government spending in order to restrain inflation and promote investment into enterprises that would produce more jobs. Barre's austerity programme included wage and price controls (although Barre later lifted price controls to encourage profits) and cuts in government subsidies. This fiscal austerity did help keep the franc strong, although that weakened the ability of French exports to compete on international markets. More importantly, Barre's programme failed to limit inflation, especially after the second oil price crisis of the late 1970s, and since corporate profits were not reinvested, unemployment continued to climb. By the time of the presidential elections of 1981, therefore, the Giscard-d'Estaing administration could claim no appreciable economic success. For that and other reasons, the French people demonstrated convincingly that they were ready for something new.

THE MITTERRAND ADMINISTRATION

Although the French Socialists had been part of many governing coalitions since the Second World War, as a party they had lacked a strong profile. Certainly compared to the Gaullists and the Communists they had no powerful base of support or even definite ideology, continuing to preach a democratic socialism whose specific content seemed to become vaguer and vaguer each year. The crisis of May 1968, in which student leaders often did not even bother to attack the Socialists because they considered them irrelevant, focused attention on the party's weakness, prompting reappraisal and reform. At the December 1971 party congress at Epinay, delegates voted to abolish the old SFIO and create a new French Socialist Party, one more attuned to the political and organisational realities of the Fifth Republic.

Epinay represented not just a political shift, but also a personal victory for François Mitterrand, who had engineered the change and became the undisputed head of the new party. Mitterrand's own life demonstrated how far the Socialists had evolved from their roots as a working-class revolutionary party. Born and raised in a conservative middle-class Catholic family, Mitterrand had studied law and political science first in the provinces, then in Paris. He fought in the war of 1940, was taken prisoner, then escaped and made his way back to France, later taking part in the Resistance. After the war he worked his way up through the political ranks in several different administrations, and in 1965 waged his first campaign for the presidency of France. He did not actually join the Socialist Party until 1971, when he became its leader. Not only did he have no real history with the party, but also he had never served in a trade union or any other working-class organisation. Moreover, as became clear near the end of his life, Mitterrand had not always been a man of the political Left. During his youth in the 1930s he had joined a fascist organisation in Paris, and before joining the Resistance during the war he had worked for Vichy, earning a major decoration from the collaborationist government. In short, François Mitterrand the Socialist politician was far more of a politician than a Socialist, and under his leadership the party would evolve in new directions.

One of Mitterrand's first acts as president of the new Socialist Party was to hammer out an alliance, the Common Programme, with the PCF. The two parties had been rivals for most of their history since the 1920s. The demise of tripartism in 1947 had created a situation where the Communists were larger and got more votes, but the Socialists were more likely to take part in national governments. The Common Programme signalled the Socialists' abandonment of their postwar inclination to look for allies among centrist parties, instead returning to the Popular Front ideal of a political coalition anchored firmly on the Left. The idea proved an attractive one to many French voters, and elections during the mid-1970s brought major triumphs for the alliance. At the same time, however, this alliance represented a calculated and ultimately successful gamble that the Socialists could replace the Communists as the pre-eminent party of the French Left. For the most part the PCF had failed to respond to the challenges posed by the young rebels of 1968. It had remained entrenched in a narrow Stalinist perspective and by the late 1970s seemed to many an aging bureaucracy out of touch with contemporary realities. Largely out of fear of being displaced, the PCF broke with the Common Programme late in 1977, further alienating many French progressives and paradoxically helping to bring about the strengthening of the Socialists they had so sought to avoid. As a result, during the parliamentary elections of 1978 the Socialists outscored the PCF, making François Mitterrand the unquestioned leader of the French Left.

On 10 May 1981, François Mitterrand was elected the fourth president of the Fifth Republic, defeating Valéry Giscard-d'Estaing by over one million votes. Mitterrand immediately responded by dissolving the National Assembly and holding new parliamentary elections, which produced an absolute Socialist majority and thus assured him of control over both executive and legislative branches of government. Mitterrand's historic election as president in 1981 was not just a victory of the Left in general, but a triumph of the Socialist Party in particular. It confirmed the Socialists' status as leading party of the Left, and marked the new power of the Left in French politics. More generally, it symbolised a departure from postwar political patterns of Gaullist dominance and a powerful but marginalised Communist Party. The significance of the Socialist victory fuelled an explosion of rejoicing throughout Paris. Crowds thronged the Champs Elysées and other major thoroughfares cheering and waving banners. Mitterrand publicly and solemnly celebrated his victory by walking alone to the Pantheon, the repository of France's illustrious dead, carrying a single red rose.

The Socialist victory at first did seem to represent a powerful new wind of change for the nation. The new government, dominated by the Socialists but also including Communist ministers, implemented a number of important reforms during its first year. In November 1981, the Justice Ministry abolished the death penalty, retiring the guillotine for good. The administration created a new ministry for women's affairs, and passed a law requiring equal pay for equal work. An even more far-reaching shift was the enactment over the next few years of a broad-ranging decentralisation policy, giving more power to mayors and departmental councils, and breaking with the tradition of centralised French government that went all the way back to Louis XIV. Under the leadership of the flamboyant, Kennedyesque Jack Lang, the Mitterrand government also carved out a dynamic new cultural policy. Lang initiated an ambitious new programme of subsidies for literally thousands of local theatres, libraries and other cultural groups, and established a national Music Festival to encourage all French men and women to exercise their musical talents. More substantially, the Mitterrand administration ended the state monopoly of radio and television, encouraging the proliferation of all sorts of 'free radio stations' and cable TV services. Not since the Popular Front had a French government shown such determination to bring culture to the masses.

This was all well and good, but the basic problem facing France was recession and unemployment. By the early 1980s nearly two million French men and women were out of work, and it was clear to most that the Mitterrand government's popularity would rise or fall on its ability to bring back the good times of the 1960s. In addressing the economic crisis the Socialists adopted a strategy combining traditional Socialist solutions with a Keynesian strategy of reflation. As a concession to both the PCF and its own left wing, the Socialist administration undertook the most comprehensive series of nationalisations since the Liberation, bringing under state control the steel industry, major electronics and armaments companies, and thirty-six of the biggest banks in the country. The Auroux Laws of 1981 not only strengthened the trade unions but also gave workers higher wages, a shorter working week, and an extra week of paid vacation, bringing the total to five per year. In addition, the government lowered the retirement age and raised both family allowances and pensions.

These policies arose out of the classic Keynesian belief that higher wages would lead to more consumer spending, thereby increasing industrial output and creating more jobs. Pumping more money into the economy would therefore lift it out of recession. So the theory ran, but in the early 1980s the Mitterrand administration's attempt to provide a progressive solution to the economic crisis failed miserably. Much of the new consumer spending went to pay for imports, thus increasing the nation's balance of payments deficit rather than benefiting French industry. The prospect of a Socialist government also triggered major capital flights out of the country, especially to Swiss banks, producing a crisis of investor confidence and weakening the franc. Above all, France attempted its Keynesian solution at a time when many other European and American governments were adopting deflationary solutions, cutting public spending and raising interest rates. As a result, both inflation and unemployment continued to increase, forcing Mitterrand to devalue the franc twice during his first year in office. The failure of the Socialist economic policy foreshadowed the dilemma of progressives in the late twentieth century era of capitalist globalisation.

Faced with this evidence that France could not exist as a socialist island in a capitalist sea, the Mitterrand administration altered its policies drastically over the next few years, abandoning many left-wing policies to embrace the logic of deflation. Between 1982 and 1984 the government enacted wage and price freezes, raised taxes, cut public expenditures and lightened the tax burden on businesses. It also abandoned its attempt to democratise secondary education by increasing state control over private schools, after the reforms proposed by Minister of Education Alain Savary brought one million protestors out onto the streets of Paris in June 1984. Shortly thereafter Mitterrand ousted Pierre Mauroy, a traditional Socialist politician, as prime minister, replacing him with Laurent Fabius. This shift was highly symbolic, for the young Fabius, an ENA (National Administration School) graduate from a wealthy background, seemed less like a Socialist and more like a bourgeois technocrat, someone who resembled Valéry Giscard-d'Estaing physically as well as politically. The new prime minister implemented further cutbacks in the public sector, in particular abandoning unprofitable industries, and enacted more business incentives. By 1986 these policies and changes in the international economy had helped tame the demons of inflation and unemployment. Nonetheless, Mitterrand's administration had achieved this at the expense of traditional Socialist ideology. Although many social benefits remained, still the most powerful left-wing government since 1947 had led a frontal attack on the proudest achievement of the Resistance, the welfare state. At this time the long heritage of the French Left seemed very remote indeed.

Politically, the government's about-face was an example of too little, too late. The Left, especially the PCF, had been steadily losing elections ever since 1983. In 1986 national elections gave a right-wing coalition a majority of seats in parliament, presenting France with a constitutional dilemma. For the first time in the history of the Fifth Republic, the presidency and the National Assembly were controlled by different political parties. This period of 'cohabitation', with Mitterrand as president and the Gaullist leader Jacques Chirac as prime minister, lasted for two years, until the presidential elections of 1988. Mitterrand won re-election and, as in 1981, immediately dissolved parliament and called for new legislative elections. The PS barely won control of the National Assembly, ending the period of cohabitation and restoring full Socialist control. Yet Mitterrand now seemed an aging leader without new ideas or grand designs, one incapable of restoring the euphoria of 1981. During his second seven-year term, from 1988 to 1995, he undertook no major new initiatives. Instead, during the 1990s the PS solidified its dominance of France's political centre, quietly presiding over the decline of the traditional Left while new issues and problems seized the public imagination.

HISTORY, MEMORY AND THE HOLOCAUST

The end of economic prosperity was not the only aspect of the postwar period that began to unravel during the Mitterrand years. One set of core beliefs that shaped national identity during the years after 1945 concerned the Nazi Occupation and Vichy collaboration. Standard historical interpretations of this period argued that most French people had supported the Resistance, either actively or passively, and had opposed German rule. This view saw the Vichy regime as a puppet government imposed upon France by Berlin, a regime with no legitimacy or roots in French history. As far as the genocide visited upon the Jews was concerned, this belief portrayed it as solely the fault of the Nazis, a foreign racism forced upon an unwilling people. The Second World War thus appeared as a triumphant, united, national struggle against fascism, combining progressive ideology and French identity. From the 1970s, however, voices both within and without France began challenging this cosy perspective, arguing that the history of occupied France was less glorious and far more complex. Like the struggles over the historiography of the French Revolution, revisionist accounts of France's wartime history arose not just out of academic disputes, but reflected broader tensions in how the French people viewed themselves as a whole.

The single most important factor in reopening the debate about Occupation France was the great 1971 documentary film, *The Sorrow and the Pity*, by Marcel Ophuls. A four-hour study of the provincial French city of Clermont-Ferrand, consisting mostly of interviews, the film clearly revealed that many French people accepted, even approved, the German Occupation and Vichy regime. Moreover, it demonstrated that wartime anti-Semitism was in fact deeply ingrained in the French people. Shortly afterwards an American historian, Robert Paxton, published a study entitled *Vichy France: Old Guard and New Order* (1972), which reinforced many of Ophuls' key arguments. Moreover, Paxton contended that the Vichy regime, far from being an alien imposition on French politics, arose out of a French right-wing tradition going back to the Dreyfus Affair of the 1890s. Both Ophuls' film and Paxton's book received great attention from the French public, provoking storms of controversy and agonised debates.

One important reason for the reassessment of Vichy France was an increased self-assertiveness and group identity among the nation's Jewish population. By the 1980s nearly 750,000 Jews lived in France, more than in any other nation in Europe outside the Soviet Union. While many individuals had made major contributions to French life, as a community they lacked visibility or political influence. There was no discernible 'Jewish vote', for example, and many French Jews lacked any strong religious identity. In the 1970s and 1980s Jewish French men and women began to speak out more forcefully, due to a variety of factors ranging from Israel's stunning victory in the 1967 war to the maturation of a new, more assertively Jewish population of Algerian origin. A rise in violent anti-Semitic incidents, notably the bombing of a Parisian synagogue in 1980, also galvanised the community. In particular, French Jews and others began pushing for a more thorough accounting of the persecution of their community during the war. As Paxton and others made clear, it was not true that the Germans simply imposed the Final Solution on France. Quite the contrary, Vichy officials had not only invented their own anti-Semitic measures, but also themselves rounded up thousands of Jews, especially foreign Jews resident in France, shipping them on a one-way journey to the concentration camps of Eastern Europe. Starting in the 1970s, the subtle postwar taboo against speaking about French anti-Semitism and the Holocaust began to unravel, as not only scholars but survivors themselves began to tell what had actually happened to the Jews of France in those years. As one woman commented fifty years after her deportation, 'I never saw a single German uniform when they took us away' (Fenby, 1999: 226–7). In the face of such testimony, it became increasingly difficult to believe in the purity of the Resistance ideal.

Changing views of Occupation and Resistance also affected national political life. In 1981 Mitterrand had been elected in part as a symbol of the continuing legacy of the Resistance, having taken part during the war while Giscard-d'Estaing's family collaborated. However, journalists gradually revealed that the president had his own dark wartime secrets, notably a history of involvement in fascist movements as a youth. In 1984, moreover, Mitterrand initiated a tradition of honouring the grave of Marshal Pétain, the leader of Vichy, a practice he repeated regularly for the rest of his presidency. By the 1990s, the old idea that one had to have a Resistance pedigree to lead the nation lay in tatters, weakened not only by the passing of years but also by the increasing ambiguity of that legacy.

The most significant, and dramatic, examples of public reassessment of the history of the Occupation were a series of highly publicised trials that took place during the 1980s and 1990s. In 1987 the French government arrested and brought to trial Klaus Barbie, the wartime head of the Gestapo in Lyons, accused in particular of deporting Jewish children from that city to their deaths. The prosecution, led by the historian and leading Nazi hunter Serge Klarsfeld, used the proceedings to lay bare the sordid history of the Holocaust in France. Barbie was duly convicted and sentenced to life imprisonment. However, Barbie was a German, and thus his trial did not depart significantly from the idea that the Nazis had wronged France as a whole. More important in this respect were the trials of Paul Touvier and Maurice Papon. Paul Touvier had headed the Vichy militia during the war, taking the lead in rounding up Jews for deportation. Initially hidden by the Catholic Church after the war and pardoned in 1971, Touvier was arrested in 1989 as further evidence of his wartime crimes surfaced. After years of legal wrangling, Touvier went to trial in 1994 for crimes against humanity. After a relatively brief trial, the Assize court of Versailles judged him guilty, making Touvier the first Frenchman to receive this verdict. Three years later came the turn of Maurice Papon, a career senior administrator who had been a Vichy official in Bordeaux during the war. Accused of complicity in the deportation of over 1,500 Jews during the war, Papon sat stony-faced during the trial and refused to admit any guilt, even after his conviction in April 1998.

The trials of Touvier and Papon in particular constituted a national crisis of conscience for France, for they demonstrated in unimpeachable detail just how widespread French complicity had been with Vichy and the Holocaust. The Papon trial in particular produced an extraordinary series of national confessions. President Jacques Chirac officially admitted the responsibility of the French state for wartime deportations of Jews. The Catholic Church also apologised for its complicity with anti-Semitism during the Occupation, followed by national organisations representing police, lawyers and other professions. For the first time since the war, therefore, France as a nation was willing to admit that the legacy of the Resistance was not the nation's only important inheritance from the war, that Vichy had also played an important part in the making of contemporary France. This important shift in the way the French remembered the war thus underlined the decline of old postwar certainties and the new character of French politics and life at the turn of the century.

IMMIGRATION, RACIAL CONFLICT AND THE RISE OF THE EXTREME RIGHT

The reconsideration of French anti-Semitism and the Holocaust during the 1980s and 1990s took place in the context of a broader resurgence of race as an issue in the life of contemporary France. Occasionally the two issues overlapped. For example, Maurice Papon had not only helped deport Jews during the Occupation, but as postwar Prefect of Police in Paris had orchestrated the massacre of Algerians in the capital during the demonstration of October 1961 (see Chapter 4). Subsequent French governments had suppressed most news of that bloody event, and it was not until Papon's trial in 1998 that the tragedy finally became public and the Chirac administration agreed to declassify official records pertaining to it. More generally, however, the rise of a new, multi-racial population in France, and the personal and political hostility frequently directed against it, seemed something very new to national life. A product of the last quarter of the twentieth century, France's new racial diversity seemed to underline the shifting nature of that society as it moved into the twenty-first century.

For a variety of reasons, questions of race in contemporary France have often been framed as problems of immigration. As noted earlier in this text, France has a very long history of immigration, and immigrants, primarily from southern Europe, made a crucial contribution to the French economy during the boom years of the 1950s and 1960s. By the mid-1970s non-white immigrants, especially from North Africa, constituted a large and growing minority of all foreign workers in France. This was the situation when the period of economic prosperity ended, creating a new situation for labour and ending the optimism of the postwar years. Even though many immigrants performed tasks disdained by French workers, they soon came to be viewed as a reason why citizens could not find jobs. In response to the crisis and rising unemployment rates, in 1974 the French government abruptly suspended all legal immigration from abroad.

While this may have been intended to reduce the numbers of non-whites in France, in fact the reverse happened over the next decades. Substantial illegal immigration persisted, especially from sub-Saharan Africa, replenishing the African culture of neighbourhoods like Barbès-Rochechouart in Paris. At the same time, under the policy known as family reunification, the government allowed some foreign workers in France to bring their wives and children to live with them. It hoped to avoid the prospect of a rootless and threatening population of single young men of colour without ties in French society. This policy not only increased the size of France's non-whites, but created new, fully-fledged communities in French cities and towns, communities that were clearly permanent. As these families grew, they made their presence felt in not only housing but also French schools, and generally in public life in ways that immigrant men had not.

By the early 1980s a major subject of discussion in French political life was the so-called 'second generation' immigrants, young people of non-European origin born in France. These young people were thoroughly French, often never having known any other country, yet were generally perceived as alien, even dangerous, by society in general. The rise to maturity of this generation coincided with the depths of the economic recession, and they were often the last hired and first fired. Many non-white families lived in the big public housing developments of the suburbs outside Paris, Lyons, and other large French cities, so that the image of the suburb, or *banlieue*, came to resemble for French people the image of the inner-city or ghetto for Americans. The combination of high unemployment, poor housing, police intolerance, and racial discrimination created an atmosphere of despair, and at times of violence. During the 1980s and early 1990s suburbs of French cities witnessed a series of riots by non-white (and often white as well) youth, involving battles with the police, the torching of automobiles and other acts of rage.

More than any other group, those of North African, especially Algerian, origin have been targeted by many as *the* racial issue in contemporary France. France today is home to between 4 and 5 million Muslims, making Islam the second largest religion in the country, and Algerians are the largest non-European ethnic group. North African Muslims have often found it difficult to integrate into French society, for a number of reasons. The bloody heritage of the Algerian war has made it difficult for some French people to welcome Algerian immigrants. Such tensions surface especially in southern France, where cities like Marseilles and Toulon contain large numbers of both Algerians and *pieds noirs*, French people who left Algeria in 1962. More generally, a deep hostility to Islam runs through French society, as in much of the Western world. Fears of Islam have deep historical roots in France, going back to the Crusades. Contemporary anxieties focus on the idea that Muslims generally refuse to assimilate into French society and constitute an alien presence. France's colonial heritage plays a role in this belief, as does the rise of Islamic fundamentalism after the Iranian revolution of 1979. The latter is seen as a threat to France's tradition of separation of church and state, and republicanism in general. In 1989 the so-called Headscarves Affair gave rise to searing national debates, when three Muslim schoolgirls in the town of Creil insisted on wearing the Muslim veil to school, in defiance of the ideal of secular public education. Some French fear that youth of North African origin, or *beurs* as they are known in local slang, will adopt fundamentalist beliefs as a political protest.

The most important result of these anxieties has been the rise of a powerful racist political movement in contemporary France. In 1972 several right-wing and neo-fascist organisations came together to create a new political party, the National Front. Led by the charismatic Jean-Marie Le Pen, a burly brawler who had served as a soldier in both the Indochinese and Algerian wars, the National Front quickly seized upon immigration as a political issue. It began attacking 'immigrants', by which it generally implied non-whites, not only for taking jobs away from French people, but more generally for constituting a mortal danger to French civilisation. In a nation increasingly wracked by economic crisis, this argument began to bear fruit. In 1984 the Front emerged as a major player in French politics when it won 11 per cent of the vote in elections to the European parliament. By the beginning of the 1990s it was winning as much as 15 per cent of the vote in national elections, and much higher vote totals in areas like Provence and the suburbs of Paris and Lyons. Twenty years after its founding, the Front was regularly attracting more electors than the declining PCF, which it had also largely replaced as the most important party of protest in France. Much credit for the Front's success must go to Le Pen himself, a natural self-promoter with a penchant for making outrageous and offensive public statements. Non-white immigrants, as well as the Front's political enemies on both Left and Right, received the brunt of his attacks. He also made periodic anti-Semitic remarks, renewing contemporary French far-Right ties to the fascist past. Above all, Le Pen and the National Front rejected any pretense of multiculturalism, taking Joan of Arc as their symbol to demonstrate their belief in traditional France.

The impact of the National Front on French politics has gone well beyond its own voters. Although the Front drew supporters from all other political parties, its effect was greatest on the traditional Right, the RPF and UDF. Consequently, in order to minimise their losses, these parties, especially the Gaullist RPF, frequently flirted with racist positions themselves. During the 1990s Gaullist governments implemented a series of measures restricting the rights of immigrants and even threatening the citizenship of young people born in France. In 1992 Gaullist leader Jacques Chirac caused an uproar by describing a typical immigrant household as '...father, three or four wives, about 20 kids, earning $10,000 a month without working...' (*The New York Times*, 18 March 1992). In 1999 the National Front split between factions headed by Le Pen and heir-apparent, Bruno Megret. Yet, by then it was clear that the issue of racism in contemporary France unfortunately went far beyond one political party.

Yet no matter how much some French people may wish for simpler times or agitate for the repatriation of immigrants, the multicultural France of today is an undeniable and irreversible fact. One need only travel to places like the Parisian suburb of Sarcelles, whose population of 58,000 includes people from sixty different countries, or the Montchovet projects in Saint-Etienne, where 70 per cent of the residents are immigrants, to realise this. Many of the tensions surrounding people of colour in contemporary France arise in fact from class conflicts, conflicts which have played an important and long-standing role in French history. The fact that such conflicts are now increasingly racialised, however, speaks to a new theme in national life. It also seems to suggest another way in which France is following American examples. Much of the hostility in France to notions of multiculturalism reflects a rejection of patterns of race relations in the United States. At the same time, many symbols of racial identity among the black and brown youth of France, from rap music to films like *La haine*, are consciously borrowed from American (especially African-American) models. For some in France, not just on the Right, the American example suggests another challenge to Republican traditions of assimilation and individuality.

In spite of the often ugly emotions this survey of race in contemporary France has revealed, it is possible to end on a positive note. For all those who support the National Front, many more people in France have been horrified by its racist rhetoric. Some have organised anti-racist groups, most notably SOS-Racism, to promote egalitarian racial and social policies. More generally, France has had more success in integrating its non-white populations than is often recognised. Racial intermarriage rates tend to be much higher than in the United States, and although many people of colour live in poor areas, France has few equivalents to the massive black ghettos of America. It is also true that people of colour have made, and continue to make, major contributions to French culture. Senegalese musicians have made 'Afropop' music one of France's most important examples of contemporary popular culture. The most pronounced recent example of this was France's joyous 1998 victory in the World Cup, featuring a team led by an Algerian, with members from Senegal and Guadeloupe. The victory, the country's first in the international football competition, produced a stunning explosion of national euphoria: 1.5 million jubilant fans crowded the Champs Elysées, creating the largest public celebration in Paris since the Liberation. One swallow does not a summer make, and a sporting triumph cannot alone erase racial tensions. Yet it is also possible that the many photographs of the triumphant World Cup team may one day seem a representation of France every bit as authentic as the Eiffel Tower or Nôtre Dame.

FRANCE AND EUROPE IN THE POST-COMMUNIST ERA

For many historians and other commentators on European affairs, the twentieth century really came to an end with the collapse of Soviet Communism during the early 1990s. The epochal events that began with the destruction of the Berlin Wall in 1989 and culminated with the dissolution of the USSR in 1991 spelled a new era not just for Russians or Germans, but for all the nations of Europe. For the French, the dawn of the post-Soviet years offered both problems and prospects. Appropriately, with the end of the Cold War division of the continent European unification became a key preoccupation during the 1990s. This rapidly escalating process held out the prospect of a new cosmopolitan spirit, as well as solid opportunities for French industry. At the same time, fears of a reunified Germany, and more generally of the loss of French national identity, created concerns among many. As the decade made clear, however, whatever difficulties the process of international integration might create in the short term, France's future lay with Europe.

France entered the 1990s with a lacklustre economy and a Socialist administration that seemed to have run out of steam. The Socialists had registered some success in reviving the French economy, but the international downturn of the early 1990s once again raised unemployment past the 10 per cent mark. By this time recession was beginning to seem endemic in France, a bitter twenty years that followed the thirty glorious ones. Moreover, the enthusiasm that had greeted the Socialist victory of 1981 and the hopes for a new day in French politics had largely disappeared. Mitterrand himself seemed to retreat from public life, earning the nickname 'the Sphinx' for his isolation and inscrutability.

One measure of the malaise was the series of scandals that shook the party and the nation in the early 1990s. One of Mitterrand's proudest achievements, decentralisation, had indeed given more power to local officials, but by removing some national controls had also allowed cronyism and corruption to flourish. The mayors of both Nice and Grenoble were convicted of financial improprieties and sent to prison in this period. Yet corruption also touched cabinet members and other national political figures, as well as members of the financial and business communities. Perhaps worst of all was the contaminated blood scandal that came to light in 1991, when the public learned that doctors at the National Centre for Blood Transfusion had used blood supplies infected with the HIV virus, thus giving AIDS to some 1,300 patients. By 1994 a popular joke in Paris ran: 'What is the difference between Nelson Mandela and the French Government? Answer: Mandela went to jail before being elected' (Ardagh, 1999: 56).

Economic and political problems produced political disaster for the Socialists. In 1993 the Right won the parliamentary elections by one of the biggest landslides in national history, electing a new National Assembly that was 80 per cent conservative. Two years later the Mitterrand era came to an end with the expiration of the Socialist leader's second term and the election of Gaullist Jacques Chirac as the new president of the French Republic. In the elections, smaller political parties, not only the National Front but also the environmentalist Green Party, did well, pointing to a general splintering of French political life. Chirac began his presidency by ignoring campaign promises to reduce unemployment, instead concentrating on a new austerity programme, slashing a wide range of social benefits. This prompted a massive wave of strikes in protest at the end of 1995, and ultimately helped the Socialists regain control of the National Assembly in the surprise elections of 1997. However, 1997 was not 1981. The new Socialist leader, Lionel Jospin, emphasised a moderate approach to the economy, abjuring nationalisations or Keynesian policies. The Socialists thus returned to their traditional position as the leader of the moderate Left in French politics, advocating not radical innovation but rather a more humane management of the vicissitudes of capitalism.

Foreign policy also emerged as a major issue during the 1990s, after taking a back seat since the death of de Gaulle. In alliance with the United States and other European countries, France took part in two wars, the Gulf War of 1991 and the 1999 bombing of Yugoslavia. But by far the most important foreign policy issue concerned relations with the rest of Europe and the future of European integration. France's relationship to the ideal of a united Europe has been complex and not always consistent. During the 1940s and 1950s France led the efforts to create the EEC and other international organisations. De Gaulle in particular believed that his nation could dominate the continent, thereby providing France with an international position equal to that of the superpowers. This, of course, depended on a firm alliance with West Germany as a junior partner, and the Paris–Bonn axis was indeed the cornerstone of postwar European diplomacy. More generally, many French leaders viewed European integration as a way to tame German nationalism by binding that nation firmly to an international community.

The end of the Cold War and German reunification changed the very significance of European integration for France. The new Germany was, at least potentially, a political and economic powerhouse, one whose size and strength dwarfed that of France. As a result, in 1989 Mitterrand and many other French people expressed scepticism about the desirability of a united Germany, seeing it as a danger to France. Yet the careful nurturing of Franco-German ties during the postwar era has largely overcome such fears, and Germany continues to enjoy a favourable image among the French people. By the early 1990s Europe began to implement specific plans for international integration, the culmination of decades of work and evolution, and even the collapse of Soviet Communism was not able to derail them. For example, a national survey in 1989 showed that 78 per cent of the French population favoured the idea of a united Europe.

The first major step took place in 1985, with the ratification by France, West Germany and the Low Countries of the Schengen Agreement, which abolished border controls between their respective countries. France delayed implementation of the agreement for a few years, in response to fears of international terrorism and drug trafficking, but did finally enact the principle by the mid-1990s. More significantly, in December 1991, the heads of state of the twelve EEC countries held a summit meeting in the Dutch town of Maastricht to hammer out plans for further European unification. The Maastricht Treaty consisted of several provisions for integration, most notably the creation of a single European currency. It had to be ratified by each nation, and Mitterrand seized the opportunity to hold a national referendum on European unification in 1992. This soon turned into France's first great debate on the merits of a united Europe. Those in favour argued that unification was the way of the future, that it would bring greater prosperity to France, and that it would effectively tie the new Germany more closely to Europe. Those opposed, who included both the Communists and the National Front, contended it would lead to the domination of France either by Germany or by the 'Eurocrats' of Brussels, and that it would benefit the wealthy at the expense of the poor. In September 1992, those in favour of Maastricht won, by the very slender margin of 51 to 49 per cent. In general, young, well-off, urban and educated France voted yes, while poor, rural and older France voted no. The nation was still of two minds about the desirability of European integration but, however gingerly, it had cast its lot with the forces of internationalism.

The next major step was the creation of a single European currency, and in this effort France again took the lead. The so-called European Monetary Union (EMU) was the brainchild of Jacques Delors, former finance minister and a deep believer in European integration. It began with the abolition of all tariffs and the creation of a united trading market in 1992, and then moved on to establish a single currency. After a lengthy series of negotiations involving the alignment of the different national economies, the Euro was born in 1999, with member nations of the EMU agreeing to phase out national currencies in the first decade of the new century. Beyond its financial and economic effects, the shift to an international banknote constitutes a powerful symbol of French and European life after 2000. The question remains to be answered, will France without the franc still be France?

Perhaps the best way to sum up the Mitterrand years is to say that during this period France's postwar era came to an end and the nation moved into a new *fin de siècle*, the eve of the twenty-first century. The election of Jacques Chirac as president in 1995 marked the first time since 1944 that the French head of state had no Resistance credentials, because he was twelve years old at the Liberation. More substantively, other characteristics of the 1980s and 1990s heralded this shift. Although since 1997 France has enjoyed an economic upturn, the Mitterrand era as a whole was dominated by stagnation, high unemployment and hard times. It was hard to foresee a renewal of the prosperity and optimism that so typified the *trente glorieuses* anytime in the near future. Reassessments of Vichy and the Holocaust called into question the belief that the Resistance represented a unified national heritage, and quarrels over race and multiculturalism challenged the ability of French identity to be both universalist and identifiably French. Moreover, the accelerating pace of European integration made some wonder if such a concept as France would continue to exist in the new millennium.

The very intensity of these debates makes it hard to argue that France lost its particular character at the end of the twentieth century, becoming merely a Western industrialised democracy like any other. Whereas the Socialists did certainly take on a more centrist tone in these years, and the PCF lost much of its strength, the rise of powerful new 'fringe' parties like the Greens and above all the National Front suggested that French political life retained a great deal of individuality. At the dawn of the new information age the French even created their own on-line network, the Minitel, which offered French citizens both benefits and liabilities with the rise of the Internet. Given both the determination of the people of France to preserve an ancient culture, and their continued desire to make it a technological and political standard bearer for other nations, it seems clear that a distinctive place called France will endure for many years to come.

PART THREE   ASSESSMENT

CHAPTER SEVEN

INTO THE NEW MILLENNIUM

If France devoted much of the first half of the twentieth century to waging war, during the second half its primary concern was building the peace. War became once again, as was true during most of the nineteenth century, something fought outside Europe, especially in the colonies. At home, in contrast, the French could concentrate on ensuring the prosperity of both individual citizens and the nation as a whole. Economic prosperity went hand in hand with technological innovation, transforming daily life in France, and the nation's intellectuals and artists continued to make major contributions to global culture. Even after the long postwar era of plenty came to an end in the 1970s, the French people continued to enjoy opportunities and a standard of living undreamed of by earlier generations. Like during the late nineteenth century, the national experience after 1945 seemed to bear out the wisdom of the old saying, 'Happy as god in France'.

This combination of peace and prosperity tempts the historian to make analogies between France in the late nineteenth and late twentieth centuries, viewing the latter era as a new *belle époque*. Yet such a comparison ultimately obscures more than it clarifies. Not only had France changed strikingly in the space of a century, but in 2000 the nation confronted challenges largely absent in 1900. Perhaps most notably, France exercised relatively less power in world affairs than it had in the late 1800s. During most of the postwar era France belonged to an international coalition dominated by a much larger and stronger nation, the United States. France's ability to retain considerable independence did not alter the basic facts of the Cold War, nor its relatively subordinate posture therein. The collapse of the Soviet Union and the end of the Cold War created new opportunities, but not for France as an individual nation. Rather, it became clear that France would exercise any influence in world affairs within the context of a united Europe, one that conceivably might be directed from Berlin, not Paris. Some French men and women at the end of the twentieth century worried that Germany might finally gain by peaceful means what it had failed to acquire by thirty years of hostility and war. Moreover, whereas at the end of the nineteenth century France was approaching the zenith of its colonial expansion, the dominant theme of the late twentieth century was decolonisation. France might retain important influence in its former dependencies, but ideas of empire had become a vanished dream.

Finally, the Second World War itself constituted a singular memory for France after 1945. Not since the Revolution had the French people known such a military and social cataclysm, and not even that event paralleled the experience of the Occupation. This study has argued that lessons drawn from the war, and in particular the consensus formed by those who fought in or valued the legacy of the Resistance, constituted a central theme for France after the Liberation. This consensus presented several advantages that accounted for its strength. It reasserted the notion of French self-determination, one called into question not only by the Occupation itself but also by the subsequent Cold War. It united two of the most potent political forces in the country, Gaullism and Communism, and in doing so underlined the importance of French unity. In the context of postwar discord, the ideal of the Resistance recalled a time when French women and men, workers and intellectuals, citizens, foreigners and colonial subjects all strove for a common goal, the rebirth of France. At the same time, the legacy of the Resistance stressed the struggle for social justice as a national and economic endeavour, rather than one based on class conflict and division. A dream that arose out of a nightmare, the spirit of the Resistance symbolised the will of the French people to endure and triumph, enabling France to carve out a brilliant future after the war.

Yet as this study has also tried to show, this ideological blueprint did not and could not endure forever. Rose-coloured images of the Resistance had served to obscure the very real disputes and ambiguities of that era; gradually as the war receded into memory, French people began to challenge its status as national foundational myth. The first major challenge arose on the margins of France, in the colonies, as Vietnamese, Algerians and other subject peoples staged revolutionary and nationalist revolts against French rule, underscoring the hypocrisy of a nation which seemed to preach universal liberty for its citizens only. The striking prosperity of the *trente glorieuses* represented a major achievement of the Resistance legacy, but the end of the economic boom underlined its inadequacy, in particular calling into question the welfare state that had been one of its proudest achievements. The massive shift of intellectuals from left-wing *engagement* to right-wing scepticism signalled the disaffection of the segment of French society most loyal to the anti-fascist ideal, while the historical reassessment of the entire Occupation experience demonstrated that Vichy and collaboration were just as French as resistance itself. Finally, to bring the circle back around to its beginnings, the disputes about race and multiculturalism posed once again the colonial challenge to the contradictions of French universalism, this time from within the heart of the nation, not its periphery.

Perhaps the most significant effect of the decline of cosy certainties about the Resistance was not so much the end of a cherished myth, but rather the absence of anything new to fill the gap it left behind. On the eve of the twenty-first century the nation once again seems unsure about what it means to be French, at a time when the concept of the nation has to confront both a new wave of assertive ethnic and racial identity, and the fundamental transformation of European integration. Combined with continued economic difficulties, this sense of national disorientation underlies much of the malaise that seems to affect so many French men and women. In a world dominated by the Internet and the Eurodollar, what special role can the people of France play? Does the nation still possess a distinctive culture, history and ideology that can bring disparate elements together in a celebration of their common heritage? Who is French, and who in the twenty-first century will want to be?

History is not prophecy, and answers to such questions lie well beyond the bounds of this study. However, let me suggest that this is not the first time the French have faced such agonising questions of self-reappraisal, and in the past they have always found a way to reassert their fundamental national identity. For example, some feared during the 1950s and 1960s that prosperity and Americanization would doom the French way of life, yet such predictions largely came to naught. The French would do well to draw heart from such cases, but they must also realise that the greatest triumphs of its history have occurred not when it retreated into its past, but when it chose to embrace the promise of the future in all its complexity and uncertainty. France must take its place as an integral part of a global future, using its own traditions to shape and at times challenge that future, while at the same time it draws on the best that the rest of the world has to offer. The new multicultural France of the twenty-first century frightens some, but it should be a source of hope and joy for the nation, for therein lies its future and its salvation.

Let the final image of this book reflect and illuminate France past, present and future. At the stroke of midnight on 1 January 2000 France joined the rest of the world in celebrating the arrival of the new millennium. It was by no means a trouble-free celebration: not only did some of the worst rainstorms of the century leave much of the nation without power, but the special clock that had been counting down the remaining seconds of the century gave out just before the big event. Nonetheless, the French managed to greet the arrival of the future with elegance and style. At the heart of the show was the Eiffel Tower, that prototypically Parisian monument built in 1889 to commemorate the hundredth anniversary of the Revolution. Precisely at the appointed hour it turned into a magnificent, awe-inspiring fountain of electric light, shooting off bolt after bolt of luminescent power visible across much of northern France. At that moment, no other people in the world outshone the French, who could justifiably claim to be a light unto all nations. For the sake of the French people, and the many contributions they can make to the peoples of the world, may it always be so.

PART FOUR DOCUMENTS

THE PROGRAMME OF THE NATIONAL COMMITTEE OF THE RESISTANCE

Published in March 1944, this manifesto of the CNR not only set forth specific goals but, more broadly, outlined the guiding spirit of the Resistance and the new France it hoped to create.

United on our goal, united as to the necessary means to reach that goal, the rapid liberation of the national territory, the representatives of the movements, groups, parties or political tendencies grouped together in the CNR proclaim that they have decided to remain united after the Liberation:

(1) In order to establish the provisional government of the Republic formed by General de Gaulle to defend the political and economic independence of the nation, re-establish the power, grandeur, and universal mission of France;

(2) In order to watch over the punishment of traitors and the eviction from administrative and professional life of all those who consorted with the enemy or who were actively associated with the policies of the collaborationist governments.

(3) In order to demand the confiscation of properties belonging to traitors and traffickers on the black market, the establishment of a progressive tax on war profits and more generally on profits realised at the expense of the people and of the nation during the Occupation, as well as the confiscation of all enemy property ...

(4) In order to assure:
   – the establishment of democracy in the broadest sense of the term, giving voice to the French people by the re-establishment of universal suffrage;
   – full freedom of thought, belief and expression...;
   – freedom of the press...;
   – freedom of assembly...;
   – the absolute equality of all citizens before the law.

(5) In order to promote indispensable reforms:

(a) *In economic affairs:*
   – the installation of a true social and economic democracy, implying the eviction of the great economic and financial conglomerates from control of the economy;
   – a rational organisation of the economy assuring the subordination of particular interests to the general interest...;
   – the nationalisation of the great monopolistic enterprises, the collective product of French labour, such as energy, the mines, insurance companies, and large banks...;
   – workers' participation in the direction of the economy.

(b) *In social affairs:*
-   the right to both labour and leisure, notably by the re-establishment and strengthening of collective bargaining;
-   significant wage increases and guarantees of wage levels that ensure all workers and their families security, dignity and the possibility of a fully human life;
-   the guarantee of national purchasing power by policies promoting currency stability;
-   the restoration of independent trade unions, with their traditional freedoms, that will play a large role in the organisation of economic and social life;
-   a complete plan for social security, concerned with guaranteeing the basic means of existence for all citizens, in all cases in which they are unable to procure these means through their own labour...;
-   retirement benefits enabling elderly workers to end their days with dignity...

Thus will be founded a new Republic which will sweep away the regime of base reaction installed by Vichy and which will give to democratic and popular institutions the effectiveness destroyed by treason and corruption before the capitulation. ...

Forward for the struggle, forward for Victory! Long live France!

'Le Programme du CNR', reproduced in Olivier Wieviorka and Christophe Prochasson, *La France du XXe siècle: documents d'histoire* (Paris, Editions du Seuil, 1994), p. 394.

DOCUMENT 2   **PARIS LIBERATED**

On 25 August 1944, the day of the liberation of Paris from the Germans, Charles de Gaulle paraded triumphantly down the Champs Elysées at the head of a million rejoicing Parisians to City Hall, where he delivered this speech.

Why should we dissimulate the emotion which grips all of us, men and women, who are here, in our home, in a Paris which has risen up to liberate itself, and has known how to do so with its own hands. No! We will not hide this profound, sacred emotion. These are moments which transcend all of our own small lives.

Paris! Outraged Paris! Broken Paris! Martyred Paris! But liberated Paris! Liberated by herself, liberated by her people with the aid of the armies of France, with the support and aid of all of France, of France engaged in struggle, of the only France, the true France, eternal France.

Well! Since the enemy which held Paris has capitulated to us, France has returned to Paris. She has returned bleeding but resolute. She has returned, enlightened by this immense lesson, but more certain than ever of her responsibilities and her rights.

I say responsibilities first because ... for the moment we are still at war. The enemy totters but he is not yet beaten. He remains on our soil. It is not enough for us, with the aid of our dear and admirable allies, to chase him from our home for us to be satisfied after all that has happened. We intend to enter his territory, as is only right, as conquerors. This is why the avant-garde of French forces has entered Paris to the sound of cannons. This is why the great French army of Italy has landed in the south of France and is rapidly advancing up the Rhone valley. This is why our brave Resistance partisans are arming themselves with modern weapons. It is for this revenge, this vengeance and justice that we continue to fight until the final day, until the day of complete and total victory. ... Long live France!

Charles de Gaulle, speech at Paris City Hall, 25 August 1944, reproduced in *Mémoires*, vol. 1, *1940–1946* (Paris: Plon, 1970), pp. 439–40.

DOCUMENT 3   INTELLECTUALS AND POLITICAL COMMITMENT

In the introduction to the very first issue of the landmark Parisian literary journal Les Temps Modernes, *Jean-Paul Sartre set forth his belief in the importance of political involvement for literary intellectuals.*

All writers of bourgeois origin have known the temptation of irresponsibility: for the last century it has been traditional in literary careers. The author rarely establishes a connection between his works and their cash value. On one side he writes, he sings, he sighs; on the other side, he is given money. Here are two apparently unrelated facts; the best one can do is to tell oneself he is being pensioned in order to sigh. Therefore he considers himself to be more like a student on scholarship than a worker who receives the price of his labour. The theoreticians of Art for art's sake and Realism have confirmed him in this opinion. Has it ever been noticed that they have the same origin and the same goal? The author who follows the teachings of the first is principally concerned with writing works that have no purpose: if they are really free of roots or meaning they seem pretty good to him. Thus he situates himself on the margins of society, or rather he takes the role of a pure consumer, just like the scholarship student. The Realist is also a consumer. As for producing, that is another matter; he has been told that science is not concerned with what is useful, and he aims for the infertile impartiality of the scholar. ...

This heritage of irresponsibility has troubled many thinkers. They suffer from a bad literary conscience, no longer really knowing whether writing is admirable or grotesque. Formerly the poet was regarded as a prophet, an honourable role; he also became at times cursed and a pariah, which still had some value. But today, he is fallen into the ranks of specialists, and it is not without a certain malaise that, when he registers at a hotel, he writes the profession of 'man of letters' after his name. ... We do not wish to be ashamed of writing, and we do not want to speak without saying anything. ... For us the writer is neither Ariel nor a Vestal virgin, he is 'in the moment', no matter what he does, marked, compromised, no matter where he goes. If, in certain eras, he uses his art to forge petty trinkets, that itself is a sign of a crisis in letters and doubtless in Society. Or it shows that the ruling classes have led him unknowingly into writing as a luxury, for fear that instead he add his weight to the troops of the revolution. ... Since the writer cannot escape, we ask that he tightly embrace his era: this is his unique opportunity, it is made for him and he for it. We regret the indifference of Balzac to the revolution of 1848, the frightened incomprehension of Flaubert faced with the Paris Commune. We are sorry for them, this constituted a permanent loss for them. We do not wish to miss anything of our era. Maybe there are better times, but this is ours; we only have this life to live, in the middle of this war, perhaps this revolution. ... I hold Flaubert and Goncourt responsible for the repression that followed the Commune, because they did not write a line to stop it. Some would say that that was not their affair. But was the trial of Calas Voltaire's problem? The condemnation of Dreyfus, was it Zola's affair? Was the administration of the Congo Gide's problem? Each of these authors, in a particular episode during his life, lived up to his responsibility as an author. The Occupation has taught us our responsibility. ...

To sum up, our intention is to collaborate to produce certain changes in our society. By that, we do not mean a change of hearts and minds: we gladly leave those concerns to authors with a specialised clientele. Without being materialist, we have never distinguished the soul from the body and we only recognise one indestructible reality, that of humanity. We place ourselves on the side of those who wish to change both the social condition of man and the conception that he has of himself. Therefore, our journal will take a position on all political and social issues. It will not do so politically, that is to say it will not ally itself with any political party, but it will attempt to extricate from such events its own idea of humanity and give advice conforming to that idea. If we can live up to our promises, if we can lead a few readers to share our views, this will not make us overly proud. We will simply be grateful for having rediscovered our professional good conscience and for the fact that, at least for us, literature again becomes what it has never ceased to be: a social function.

Jean-Paul Sartre, 'Presentation', *Les Temps Modernes*, October 1945, pp. 1–8.

DOCUMENT 4   CONTINUED HARDSHIPS IN FRANCE

In her journal entry of 2 April 1948, American journalist Janet Flanner reported that, although material conditions had improved in France since the Liberation, the country still had a long way to go to achieve full economic health or political consensus.

On the surface, France has improved so much in the last six months that all that is lacking is the belief that the vital, invisible underpinnings of state and society can hold the improvements in place. The average Frenchman can now find in the shops nearly everything he wants except the means of paying for it. In midtown Paris shop windows, perfect taste, which is the supreme French luxury, has at last reappeared. On the farms, the hedges have been trimmed and the ditches have been cleaned out, the farmers having profited from what may be the last year of German-prisoner farm labor. By day, in the limpid spring sunshine, Paris looks her old, beautiful self, reclining full length in the greenery by the Seine. By night, the city is lighted but largely deserted; restaurants are half empty and cafés are closed for lack of clients. Parisians dine at home, on soup, and go to bed. The rise in the birth rate here may be accidentally patriotic, but it is also alarming, considering the world shortage of food. Since the recent freeing of the franc and of the prices of most edibles and other goods, the frantic black-market bustle for necessities to eat and wear has quieted down. Paris is hovering around a new norm; the new heavy tax increases, the special fiscal levies, and the seizure of five-thousand-franc notes have combined to produce an odd, un-Gallic stoicism that is a substitute for morality. The anti-inflationary government, still insisting that the sellers' margin of profit is too wide, is using pressure to hold retail prices down, and has made a first public example of the vegetable marketman. In the spinach basket in his grocery shop or on his lettuce cart by the curb, he is forced to placard his cost price as well as his selling price. The fixers and the middlemen in the gray market – the nibblers rather than the producers – are the only business groups making big money. Factory workers say that wages must go up; factory owners say that prices cannot come down any farther without economic suicide. For political reasons, both sides exaggerate their difficulties, which are nevertheless real, and which are opposite. It is this absolute dia-metricism that is cutting France into two bleeding, anemic, and perhaps impermanent parts.

Many important items are still rationed. Except for doctors, taxi-drivers, and other specialists, the French do not get a drop of gasoline. Because the government acutely needs tourist dollars, gasoline flows in fountains for American tourists, as well as for abashed American journalists (French journalists get nearly none), for whom the liberated franc makes life nice and cheap anyway. The French operate on costly black-market gasoline coupons that trickle down from the Brittany fishing ports, where fishermen make more money by selling them than by putting out to sea in the motorboats and catching fish. The farmers also oblige, by selling the tractor-gasoline coupons. Parisian adults have had no butter ration since Christmas and this month their quarter-pound coffee ration is to be skipped, but they received a government Easter present – a rationed tin of sardines, at thirty times the prewar price. Wine is finally unrationed, but some of it is watered, or what the French call baptised, wine and spoils quickly. Compared with conditions a half year ago, there is more choice in everything and more comfort everywhere, except in the average French pocketbook. France is in a curious, momentarily excellent position of recovery. The goods are here, but the marts need faith and buyers with cash. There is a lot of intelligent skepticism as to what tomorrow and tomorrow will be in France, in Europe, and on this earth. France is like someone who has unexpectedly climbed a very high hill and stands breathless and poised on the crest.

Janet Flanner, *Paris Journal, 1944–1955* (New York: Harcourt, Brace and Co., 1965), pp. 82–3.

DOCUMENT 5   THE POLITICS OF THE LEFT BANK

In this response to Arthur Koestler's Darkness at Noon, *which revealed to the French the sordid history of Stalin's purge trials, philosopher Maurice Merleau-Ponty argues that the West is just as guilty of using violence and terror to achieve its political ends.*

Communism cannot be justified simply by showing that violence is a component of Western humanism as an historical force, since it still has to be known whether Communist violence is, as Marx thought, 'progressive'. Far less does violence provide communism with that spineless assent which pacifism, whether it means to or not, historically gives to violent regimes. But this means depriving Western politics of that wonderfully clear conscience which is so remarkable in much of contemporary Anglo-Saxon writing. It puts the debate between the Western democracies and communism into its proper domain, which is not a debate between the Yogi and Commissar but between one Commissar and another. If the events of the last thirty years lead us to doubt that the world proletariat is about to unite, or that proletarian power in one country establishes reciprocal relations among men, they in no way affect the truth of that other Marxist idea that no matter how real and precious the humanism of capitalist societies may be for those who enjoy it, it does not filter down to the common man and does not eliminate unemployment, war, or colonial exploitation. Consequently, when set against the history of all men, like the freedom of the ancient city, it is the privilege of the few and not the property of the many. How do we answer an Indochinese or an Arab who reminds us that he has seen a lot of our arms but not much of our humanism? Who dares to say that, after all, humanity has always progressed in the hands of a few and been sustained by its delegates and that we are that elite and the rest have only to wait their turn? Yet this would be the only honest reply. But this would mean acknowledging that Western humanism is a *humanism of comprehension* – a few mount guard around the treasure of Western culture; the rest are subservient. It would imply that in the end Western Humanism has nothing in common with a *humanism in extension*, which acknowledges in every man a power more precious than his productive capacity, not in virtue of being an organism endowed with such and such a talent, but as a being capable of self-determination and of situating himself in the world.

In its own eyes Western humanism appears as the love of humanity, but for the rest of men it is only the custom and institution of a group of men, their password and occasionally their battle cry. The British Empire did not send Yogi missions into Indonesia, any more than the French in Indochina, to teach 'change from within.' Their intervention in these countries has involved, to say the least, a 'change from without' and a rough one. If the reply is that their forces are defending freedom and civilization, this implies a renunciation of absolute morality and entitles the Communists to say that their forces are defending an economic system which will put an end to man's exploitation of man. It is from the conservative West that communism received the notion of history and learned to relativise moral judgment. It has not forgotten the lesson and has sought, at least in a given historical milieu, those forces which on balance have a chance of making humanity a reality. If one does not believe that the proletariat can acquire power or that it can deliver what Marxism expects of it, then perhaps those capitalist civilisations which despite their imperfections have at least the merit of existing represent the least of history's horrors. But then the difference between them and the Soviet enterprise is not the difference between heaven and hell or between good and evil; it is only a matter of the different uses of violence. Communism should be thought about and discussed as an attempt to solve the human problem and not be treated as an occasion for heated argument. It is a definite merit of Marxism and an advance in Western thought to have learned to confront ideas with the social functions they claim to articulate, to compare our perspective with others, and to relate our ethics to our politics. Any defense of the West which forgets these truths is a mystification.

Maurice Merleau-Ponty, *Humanism and Terror* (Boston, MA: Beacon, 1969), pp. 175–77.

*In this 1957 interview, philosopher and writer Albert Camus rejected the
idea of absolute truth and challenged France's leftist intellectuals to
confront their own political biases.*

The truth is that no nation has a monopoly on peace. ... Hence we shall say
that some nations are merely more bellicose than others. It seems, if I can
believe the progressive newspapers (which previously thought or said the
opposite), that America has been less bellicose than Russia of late. But there
is no need for anyone to show us that socialism can, quite as well as
capitalism, foment wars. All it takes is a little will power, and there is
scarcely any nation without that (except for those which have no army, and
even then you can't be sure). This wasn't known before simply because
there was no socialist state. Now we know. Alienation is in any case too
noble a word to describe the attitude of those who insist on seeing nothing
but doves in the East and vultures in the West. Blindness, frenzy of the
slave, or nihilistic admiration of force seems to me a more exact term. ...
Expediencies must be examined to see the dose of truth they contain, the
lesson to be drawn from them in order to correct what had previously been
thought right. But they cannot be given an advantage over the pursuit of
factual truths. Above all, we cannot grant expediency any precedence over
regard for truth, as the Communists do and the Leftist intellectuals who
follow them, for such systematic relativism leads to the death of intelligence
and the oppression of the worker. A press or a book is not true because it is
revolutionary. It has a chance of being revolutionary only if it tries to tell
the truth. We have a right to think that truth with a capital letter is relative.
But facts are facts. And whoever says that the sky is blue when it is gray is
prostituting words and preparing the way for tyranny. ... We must admit
that today conformity is on the Left. To be sure, the Right is not brilliant.
But the Left is in complete decadence, a prisoner of words, caught in its
own vocabulary, capable merely of stereotyped replies, constantly at a loss
when faced with the truth, from which it nevertheless claimed to derive its
laws. The Left is schizophrenic and needs doctoring through pitiless self-
criticism, exercise of the heart, close reasoning, and a little modesty. Until
such an effort at re-examination is well under way, any rallying will be
useless and even harmful. Meanwhile, the intellectual's role will be to say
that the king is naked when he is, and not to go into raptures over his
imaginary trappings. ...

In conclusion, I believe (as people say: I believe in God, creator of heaven
and earth) that the indispensable conditions for intellectual creation and
historical justice are liberty and the free confronting of differences. Without

freedom, no art; art lives only on the restraints it imposes on itself, and dies of all others. But without freedom, no socialism, either, except the socialism of the gallows.

Interview in *Demain*, 21–17 February 1957, reproduced in Albert Camus, *Resistance, Rebellion, and Death* (New York: Vintage, 1960), pp. 166–71.

DOCUMENT 7 ON THE OPPRESSION OF WOMEN

In her landmark text on the condition of women, The Second Sex, *Simone de Beauvoir considers the ways in which masculine domination is related to other forms of social oppression and control.*

The category of the *Other* is as original as consciousness itself. In the most primitive societies, in the most antique mythologies one always finds the duality of the Self and the Other. ... No collectivity ever defines itself as One without immediately posing the Other in opposition to itself. One only needs to bring together by chance three travellers in a railway compartment to see them view all the rest of the travellers as vaguely hostile 'others'. For the villager, all people who do not belong to his village are suspicious 'others'; for the resident of a country, the inhabitants of other lands seem like 'strangers' to him; Jews are 'others' for the anti-Semite, blacks for American racists, natives for colonial settlers, workers for the propertied classes ... often it is numerical inequality that confers this privilege: the majority imposed its law upon the minority or persecutes it. But women are not, like the blacks of America or the Jews, a minority: there are as many women as men on earth. Frequently as well two groups had been independent of each other, living in ignorance of each other, until a historical event subordinated the weaker to the stronger: the Jewish diaspora, the introduction of slavery to America, and colonial conquests are all historical facts. In these cases, for the oppressed there was a *before*: they have in common a history, a tradition, sometimes a religion or culture. In this sense the similarity established by Bebel between women and the proletariat would seem the most likely: neither are the workers a minority, nor have they ever constituted a separate collectivity. Nevertheless ... the proletariat has not always existed, but there have always been women. They are women by their physiological structure. Throughout all of history they have always been subordinate to men; their dependence is not the consequence of an event or a process, they have not *arrived*. It is in part because it escapes the accidental character of the historical fact that alterity appears here as an absolute fact. A situation created over time can change in another time, as the blacks of Haiti, among others, have demonstrated; on the contrary, it seems that a natural condition defies change. In reality, however, nature is no more immune to change than historical reality, ... Workers say 'us'. Blacks also. They regard themselves as subjects, changing the bourgeois and whites into 'others'. Women – except in the case of certain conferences which remain abstract examples – don't say 'us'; men say 'women' and women take up this word to designate themselves, but they don't really characterise themselves as a Subject. The workers made a revolution in Russia, the blacks in Haiti, the Indochinese are fighting in Indochina: the action of women has never been anything but symbolic, they have only won what men decided to give them; they have not taken anything, they have only been given. They lack the concrete means to unite themselves in a collectivity which would create women by creating a sense of the Other. They have no past, no history, no religion which belongs to them alone; they lack the solidarity of labour and interests that unites workers; they don't even have that spatial proximity that brings Jews and American blacks together in ghettos, or that makes the workers of Saint-Denis or the Renault factories a community. They live dispersed among men, attached by residence, labour, economic interest, and social condition to certain men – father or husband – more closely than to other women. ... The link which unites woman to her oppressors is comparable to no other. The division of the sexes is in effect a biological given, not a moment in human history. It is at the heart of an original *mitsein* [togetherness] that their opposition exists, and she has not broken it. The couple is a fundamental unity whose two halves are ranged against each other; no cleavage of society by sex is possible. It is this that is the fundamental characteristic of woman: she is the Other at the heart of a totality whose two halves are necessary to each other.

Simone de Beauvoir, *Le Deuxième Sexe*, vol. 1 (Paris: Gallimard, 1949), pp. 16–19.

DOCUMENT 8   **THE WAR IN INDOCHINA FROM THE PERSPECTIVE OF A VIETNAMESE FAMILY**

In her memoir of life in Vietnam from 1940 to 1975, Nguyen Thi Thu-Lam describes how opposition to French rule both galvanized and divided her middle-class Vietnamese family at the start of the Indochina war.

As the nationalist fervor grew, the French took steps to dampen it. One way to demoralize and disperse would-be revolutionaries was to bribe minor Vietnamese officials and government workers with opium, champagne, and all-night orgies. Saigon became notorious as a Babylon. While this policy diverted some segments of the population, many others were organising in small resistance groups. The French would then have pro-French Vietnamese infiltrate those groups: in that way they found out who the leaders were.

After that, it was simple enough to round them up and kill them, sometimes beheading them in public. As more resistance groups kept appearing, the authorities continued this pattern of persuasion. Reports of French atrocities fanned the flames of nationalism, and even those who opposed the Viet Minh's Communist ties saw no alternative other than a commitment to the revolution.

Father's attempt to reach the North had been complicated by the fact that our family was so large and the children were so young. In order to ensure the success of our escape from Saigon, he had finally decided to split the family in two. Mother would go on ship to Haiphong Harbor with Lan, their oldest daughter still at home, Ty, our adopted sister, and Ha and Dong, the babies. Father would take Xuan and me by train. We would all regroup in the North. Xuan and I arrived in Hanoi with Father in late 1946. On the train Xuan and I cried all the way, afraid that we would never see Mother again. Father could only try over and over to reassure us that we would soon find her, knowing that many families like ours were never reunited.

As the days turned into weeks, we still had no sign of Mother. Xuan and I no longer cried. We were staying with our cousins who made sure we were too busy for such things. They had a big house in Hanoi, once belonging to my uncle who had died of tuberculosis. His wife and daughter had also died, so his three unmarried sons now owned the house. Since we were their closest living family members, they were happy to have us. ... Though united as a family, my cousins argued constantly and bitterly about politics. Even at six, I was disturbed by their wrangles.

Hac, the oldest, followed the nationalist movement, but he belonged to a political group not aligned with the Viet Minh. Highly regarded in his profession, he had become the personal dentist of some of the Viet Minh leaders, including Ho Chi Minh, whom he personally liked. Though he questioned certain ideas of those men whose teeth he cared for, he felt the Viet Minh was the only group with enough leadership to defeat the French. Since the goal was independence, he felt duty-bound to render his services. Besides, he admired Uncle Ho and his closest aides, so he put aside his political disagreements, trusting that the Viet Minh would mend its ways after the colonialists were gone.

Hac's brother Quang, on the other hand, was an active member of the Communist Party, serving the revolutionary forces as a medical doctor. Long, the youngest, was only nineteen at the time and had not yet finished college. Like Hac, he followed the national movement, but he belonged to a vehemently anti-Communist party and had no doubt that the Viet Minh would bring Vietnam to communism.

One day, when Father was away, the three brothers started one of their typical squabbles. Hac had just read an article in the newspaper. 'You see,' he said, 'I told you so. We have to work for independence without resort to violence. The country needs us. We can't sell out to the Communists.'

'I thought that you liked Ho Chi Minh. After all, you're his personal dentist. You see a side of him no one else does!'

'You're right. I do like Uncle Ho and I do think that in some ways he's a very shrewd leader. But I deplore the tactics of the men under him!'

'I tell you,' Quang said, 'the only way this country will survive is if we all stand behind the revolutionaries. We desperately need a change. We must back Ho Chi Minh. He's our only hope against the French.'

Then Long joined in: 'I say this country has seen too much bloodshed already. The Communists will only make it worse. They're our true enemies... '.

The argument went on until one of the brothers slammed his fist on the dining table. The soup dishes clattered, and then one of the men picked up a plate and hurled it at another. Soon, the three brothers were raging at one another, throwing the dishes from the table against the wall one by one.

'You spineless dog!'

'You idiot!'

'You mindless follower!'

'You Red!'

Crouching in a corner, my sister and I began to cry. For a minute, the three looked at us and paused – momentarily shocked by their own behavior. But then they started again, yelling and pounding their fists and throwing dishes down upon the floor, every restraint in them broken. Finally, Hac, the oldest brother, caught himself. Seeing how scared we were, he walked away from the table and came to us, kneeling beside us. 'We were merely having an argument,' he said. 'We were very angry and we behaved badly. Like naughty children. Forgive us for scaring you.' The two other brothers turned and walked away, each to his own room. Led by Hac, we left the room, stepping gingerly around the broken pottery. Looking at the broken cups, hand-painted by my late aunt, I cried once again. All that beauty lost. All that waste. To me it was like stepping over the bones of my very family. But I learned quickly: that is the way with civil wars. You fight your very own family.

Nguyen Thi Thu-Lam, *Fallen Leaves: Memoirs of a Vietnamese Woman* (New Haven, CT: Yale Southeast Asia Studies Center, 1989), pp. 41–3.

DOCUMENT 9   THE FRENCH ARMY IN ALGERIA

In his memoir of his experiences as a lieutenant drafted into the French Army during the Algerian war, Jean-Jacques Servan-Schreiber demonstrates how French soldiers ultimately came to see all Algerians, not just the activists of the FLN, as the enemy.

He was a cautious fellow who almost never talked about serious things. Nobody knew his opinions – which was why people rather mistrusted him, for he was skillful at concealing them behind a disarmingly amusing façade. This time he did not seem so comfortable as usual. When he spoke up, it was in a rather solemn voice that surprised and silenced everyone else.

'Excuse me for butting in. I only wanted to suggest that if Arabs are killed by our men and no arms are found on them, you can't rule out the possibility that the victims aren't *fellagha* [FLN guerrillas] but may be honest guys from the village – which wouldn't do much good to our relations with the population.'

This cautious language did not quite make his point.

'What are you trying to say?' asked Henry.

'I'm trying to say that perhaps we were wrong to kill them. I'm trying to say that if they're fathers of families – that does happen, even with them – their wives and their children are going to miss them. That if they're sons, their mothers are going to cry. And that whether they're fathers, brothers, or sons, their death at our hands will inevitably stoke up hatred against us. I'm suggesting that it's bad business to kill people who may be innocent, and that it's not what we're here for. Once more, all my apologies. I know that since I wasn't in Indochina and I've only been in Algeria a few days, I ought to just listen.'

Thus for the first time Captain Julienne said what he felt. Everyone at the table felt a little uncomfortable. Not that they thought he was right.

Julienne was wrong, and he would find it out pretty quick. The *fellagha* are not, more's the pity, beings apart, marked with a cross on the forehead. The *fellagha* are anyone, anywhere. To get a real one you have to round up – or to kill – four or five, at least. Or to give up hunting the *fellagha*. But, in that case, what are we doing in Algeria?

'My dear sir,' said Martin, addressing Julienne with a condescending but friendly manner, 'you're right, a hundred per cent right – in theory. Unfortunately, in practice you'll find that you're faced with a choice. Either you consider *a priori* that every Arab, in the country, in the street, in a passing truck, is innocent until proved guilty – and allow me to tell you that if that's your attitude you'll get your men bumped off, the *fellagha* will be cocks of the walk, and, as for you, you'll be transferred immediately because the parents of the conscripts you'll get killed won't like it and will write to their deputies [parliamentary representatives] that you're a butcher – or you do your duty honorably, which is to say you put the *fellagha* out of commission and look after our men the best you can. In that case, there's only one way: treat every Arab as a suspect, a possible *fellagha,* a potential terrorist – because that, my dear sir, is the truth. And don't come back at me with words like *justice* and *charity.* They have nothing to do with it. I don't say they don't exist: I say all that's not in the same boat. You can talk about that in Paris with the politicians who got us into this mess. But once you're here, raising problems of conscience – and presuming the innocence of possible murderers – is a luxury that costs dear, that costs men, my dear sir, young men, innocent too, our men. I don't think you'll need more than a fortnight to see it.'

Outside, in the nighttime silence of the curfew, only the abrupt sound of short bursts from automatic arms, near or far, beat a regular rhythm. The armored patrol that scoured the country in the evening had made it a rule never to come back without 'emptying its magazines.' Everything that stirs is suspect.

Everyone was watching Captain Julienne. His black eyes, under their heavy, graying eyebrows, wandered around the table. Doubtless he felt that he had spoken a little rashly; he was alone.

Jean-Jacques Servan-Schreiber, *Lieutenant in Algeria* (New York: Alfred A. Knopf, 1957),

pp. 31–3.

DOCUMENT 10   FRENCH INTELLECTUALS PROTEST THE ALGERIAN WAR

In September 1960, in response to the trial of a French group accused of aiding the FLN, 121 prominent intellectuals published the following manifesto condemning the war in Algeria and upholding the right of all men and women to resist injustice.

A very important movement is developing in France, and it is necessary that French and international opinion be better informed about it, at a time when the new course of the war in Algeria should lead us to see, not to forget, the depths of the crisis that began there six years ago.

In ever greater numbers, French men and women have been arrested, imprisoned and convicted for having refused to participate in this war, or for having come to the aid of the Algerian combattants. Misrepresented by their adversaries ... their reasons have generally remained misunderstood. It is nonetheless insufficient to say that this resistance to public authority is respectable. A protest of men acting out of a sense of betrayed honour and a defence of the truth, its significance transcends the circumstances in which it has arisen, something important to understand no matter how things turn out.

For the Algerians, the struggle, pursued by either military or diplomatic means, is straightforward. It is a war of national independence. But what is it for the French? It is not a foreign war. The national territory of France has never been threatened. More than that, it is a war waged against men whom the State pretends to consider French, but who are themselves fighting precisely for the right to stop being French. It would not even be enough to label it a war of conquest, an imperialist war, accompanied in addition by racism. ... In fact, by a decision which constitutes a fundamental abuse of power, the government has drafted large numbers of citizens for the sole end of achieving what it itself calls a police action against an oppressed population, which has only revolted out of a desire for basic dignity, since it demands finally to be recognised as an independent community.

Neither war of conquest, nor war of 'national defence', nor civil war, the Algerian war has little by little fallen under the control of the Army itself, of a caste which refuses to give way in the face of an uprising which even civil authorities, taking into consideration the general collapse of colonial empires, seem ready to recognise.

It is today principally the will of the Army which maintains this criminal and absurd combat, and this Army, through the political role played by its leading representatives, acts sometimes overtly and violently outside the law, betraying the goals conferred upon it by the nation as a whole, compromises and risks the perversion of the nation itself, by forcing citizens under its command to act in complicity with its debased and rebellious policies. Must we remind our readers that, fifteen years after the destruction of the Hitlerian order, French militarism, in response to the demands of this war, succeeded in restoring torture and once again making of it a European institution?

It is in these conditions that many French have come to question the meaning of traditional values and obligations. What is civic responsibility when, in certain circumstances, it becomes a shameful surrender? Aren't there cases where saying no is a sacred duty, where 'treason' means the courageous respect of the truth? When, because of those who use it as an instrument of racist or ideological domination, the Army takes a position of overt or latent revolt against democratic institutions, doesn't the idea of a revolt against the Army take on a new sense?

The issue of conscience has been posed since the beginning of the war. To the extent that the war continues, it is normal that this issue of conscience be resolved concretely by ever more numerous acts of insubordination, of desertion, as well as acts of protection and aid to the Algerian fighters. Free movements which have arisen on the margins of all the official political

parties, without their assistance and, ultimately, in spite of their dis-
approval. Once more, in the absence of officials and established slogans, a
resistance has been born through a spontaneous awakening of consciousness, one that searches for and invents new forms of action and means of
struggle in the context of a new situation that political groups and
newspapers have agreed (either by inertia, ideological timidity, national or
moral prejudices) not to recognise the meaning and the true requirements.

The undersigned. ... declare:

-   We respect and consider justified the refusal to take up arms against
    the Algerian people.
-   We respect and judge justified the conduct of French people who
    consider it their duty to bring aid and protection to the Algerians,
    oppressed in the name of the French people.
-   The cause of the Algerian people, which is making a decisive
    contribution to the ruin of the colonial system, is the cause of all
    free men.

'Le Manifeste des 121', 6 September 1960, cited in Wieviorka et Prochasson, *La France du*
XXe siècle., pp. 495–9.

DOCUMENT 11   THE RISE OF CONSUMER CULTURE IN THE 1960S

In his 1965 novel Things *writer Georges Perec describes the new prosperity*
of the postwar era and its impact on an ambitious young couple. Although
widely read as an attack on consumer culture, the book is more concerned
with showing the opportunities it offered the French and the ways it
changed their society.

Jérôme was twenty-four and Sylvie twenty-two. They were both market
researchers. Their work, which was not exactly a trade nor quite a profession, consisted of interviewing people by various different techniques, on
a range of subjects. It was difficult work, requiring at the very least a high
degree of nervous concentration, but it was not uninteresting, not at all
badly paid, and it left them an appreciable amount of free time.

Like almost all their colleagues, Jérôme and Sylvie had become market
researchers by necessity and not by choice. No-one knows, in any case,
where the untrammelled development of their natural inclinations towards
idleness would have led them. There again, history had chosen for them. Of
course, like everyone else, they would have liked to give themselves to
something, to feel in themselves some powerful need that they would have
called a vocation, an ambition that would have raised them up, a passion
that would have fulfilled them. But they possessed, alas, but a single
passion, the passion for a higher standard of living, and it exhausted them.

When they were students the prospect of a mediocre degree and then a teaching post with a tiny salary at Nogent-sur-Seine, Château-Thierry or Etampes terified them so much that virtually on meeting each other ... and without needing to talk it over, they dropped out of courses they had never really begun. The thirst for knowledge did not torture them. For more prosaically, and without hiding from the fact that they were probably making a mistake and that sooner or later they would come to regret it, they thirsted for a slightly bigger room, for running hot and cold water, for a shower, for meals more varied, or just more copious, than those they ate in student canteens, maybe for a car, for records, holidays, clothes.

Motivation research had emerged in France several years earlier. That year it was still expanding fast. New agencies were springing up by the month, out of nothing, or almost. You could get work in them easily. Most often it involved going into parks or standing at school gates or knocking on doors in suburban housing estates to ask housewives if they had noticed some recent advertisement and what they thought of it. These instant surveys, called minitests or quickies, earned a hundred francs each. It wasn't much, but it was better than baby-sitting, working as a night watchman or as a dishwasher, better than any of the other menial jobs – distributing leaflets, book-keeping, timing radio advertisements, hawking, cramming – which were traditionally the preserve of students. And then the very youth of the agencies themselves, their almost informal state of development, the still total absence of trained staff, held out the prospect, at least potentially, of rapid promotion and a dizzying rise in status. ... And so for four years and maybe more they explored and interviewed and analysed. ... There was washing, drying, ironing. Gas, electricity and the telephone. Children. Clothes and underclothes. Mustard. Packet soups, tinned soups. Hair: how to wash it, how to dry it, how to make it hold a wave, how to make it shine. Students, fingernails, cough syrup, typewriters, fertilisers, tractors, leisure pursuits, presents, stationery, linen, politics, motorways, alcoholic drinks, mineral water, cheeses, jams, lamps and curtains, insurance and gardening. *Nil humani alienum*. ... Nothing that was human was outside their scope.

For the first time they earned some money. They did not like their work; could they have liked it? But they did not dislike it a great deal either. They felt they were learning a lot from it. Year after year it changed them completely.

These were their great days of conquest. They had nothing; they were discovering the riches of the world.

For years they had been absolutely anonymous. They dressed like students, that is to say badly. Sylvie had a single skirt, ugly jumpers, a pair of cord trousers, a duffle-coat; Jérôme had a mucky parka, an off-the-peg suit, one pitiful necktie. They leapt ecstatically into fashionable English clothes. They discovered knitwear, silk blouses, shirts by Doucet, cotton voile ties, silk scarves, tweed, lambswool, cashmere, vicuna, leather and jerseywool, flax and, finally, the great staircase of footwear leading from Churches to Westons, from Westons to Buntings and from Buntings to Lobbs.

Their dream was a trip to London. They would have split their time between the National Gallery, Saville Row and a particular pub in Church Street which had stuck with feeling in Jérôme's memory. But they were not yet rich enough to kit themselves out from top to toe in London. In Paris, the first money gaily earned by the sweat of their brows, Sylvie spent on shopping: a knitted silk bodice from Cornuel, an imported lambswool twin-set, a straight, formal skirt, extremely soft plaited leather shoes, and a big silk headscarf with a peacock-and-foliage pattern. Jérôme, for his part, though he was still fond of shuffling around from time to time in clogs, unshaven, wearing an old collarless shirt and denim trousers, went in for total contrasts and discovered the joys of lazy mornings: taking a bath, shaving very close, sprinkling *eau-de-toilette*, slipping on over still damp skin a shirt of unimpeachable whiteness, tying a woollen or silken necktie. He bought three of these, at Old England, together with a tweed jacket, some marked-down shirts and a pair of shoes he thought he would not be embarrassed to wear.

Then – and this was one of the most important days of their lives – they came across the Flea Market. Splendid, long-collared, button-down Arrow and Van Heusen shirts, at that time unfindable in Paris shops but which American comedy films were making increasingly popular (at least for that marginal set of people who delight in American comedies) were to be found there in untidy heaps, alongside allegedly indestructible trench coats, skirts, blouses, silk dresses, hide jackets and soft leather moccasins. They went every fortnight, on Saturday mornings, for a year or more. ...

They were changing, becoming other people. It wasn't so much because of their (nonetheless genuine) need to differentiate themselves from the people it was their job to interview, to impress without overwhelming them. Nor was it because they met a lot of people, because they were taking their leave, for ever, or so they thought, from what had been their milieu. But money – and this point cannot but be an obvious one – creates new needs. They would have been surprised to realise, if they had thought about it for a moment – but in those years they didn't think – to what extent their views of their own bodies had altered, and, beyond that, their vision of everything that affected them, of everything that mattered, of everything that was in the process of becoming their world.

Georges Perec, *Things: Story of the Sixties* (Boston, MA: David Godine, 1990), pp. 35–41.

DOCUMENT 12   FRENCH IMAGES OF AMERICA

In his tremendously successful book The American Challenge *Jean-Jacques Servan-Schreiber discusses the reasons for America's economic success, using them to point out deficiencies in French traditions.*

Americans are not more intelligent than other people. Yet human factors – the ability to adapt easily, flexibility of organisations, the creative power of teamwork – are the key to their success. Beyond any single explanation, each of which has an element of truth, the secret lies in the confidence of the society in its citizens. This confidence often seems rather naïve to Europeans, but America places it both in the ability of its citizens to decide for themselves, and in the capacity of their intelligence. ... This optimism which marks every aspect of American life is expressed in the confidence in universal suffrage for direct election of the President. We find the same confidence in the authority delegated to local government to administer everyday aspects of life and to make decisions in the fields of city planning, health, and education – decision-making powers our central government would be terrified to put into the hands of elected officials. We see it again in the catalytic role of research, where ideas are not ornaments but tools to change the world. And nothing is more *profitable* than a good idea. In the United States adult education is considered an investment, not a form of humanitarianism. ...

All clichés to the contrary, American society wagers much more on human intelligence than it wastes on gadgets. As we have seen, scientific studies are beginning to confirm what intuition led us to suspect: *this wager on man is the origin of America's new dynamism.* Despite important changes over the past 20 years, European society, particularly in France, presents a very different picture.

France is without doubt the country where people are most suspicious of their neighbors. ... Despite the prestige enjoyed by intellectuals in France, and despite the cult of Cartesian rationality, in reality there exists an evident contempt for ideas, or at least for their practical application. This is manifested as much in industry by the underdevelopment of research as in government by the scarcity of administrative research services and above all by a lack of interest in them. Best to avoid these 'dead-ends' if you have career ambitions. In both business and government, brain power is badly integrated into the organization.

This skepticism toward man's potential is common to both the Left and the Right, but it involves opposite conclusions. On the Right it leads to the sanctification of the 'natural laws of the market.'. ... It is striking that conservatives are more attached to the fetters which the pure market economy imposes on the collective will than to the freedoms it provides for individual initiative. Even today they are apt to ask the government simultaneously to release them from the discipline of the Plan and also, by closing professions or frontiers, to spare them the risks of competition. ...

On the Left the same distrust of man leads to a cult of coercive planning. Many 'progressives' still dream of setting up a society where an omniscient bureaucracy, the repository of moral order, will dictate to consumers the enlightened decisions they are incapable of making for themselves. To listen to them, it would seem that the mass of people want only to make their hovels more ugly and their cars more beautiful, that the real reason for the housing crisis is not so much the rigidity of rent control and the chaos of the real estate market as an insatiable popular appetite for immediate pleasures, intensified by a docile obedience to advertising. The Left neglects to seek remedies in better information and more effective competition that would lead to increased freedom. It has got into the habit of reinforcing regulations and putting economic activities under rigid control.

When they speak of the excesses of 'the consumer society,' many intellectuals of the older generation are really attacking the consumer's right to determine his own needs. The condemnation of this small, but precious, aspect of economic democracy indicates a resurgence of 'enlightened despotism.' An elite convinced of its own wisdom is certain it has the right to impose its own preferences through specific restraints. It would even be ready, so it says, to *restore poverty* in order to protect the masses against the *moral* risks of growth in an atmosphere of freedom. ...

These two currents of Right and Left, one sanctifying the market economy from distrust of the audacities of the Plan, the other making a controlled economy an end in itself from fear of the freedoms of the marketplace, combine into a negative 'colbertism,' centralist and suspicious of the government. Its behavior is characterized by lack of a coherent design for the whole, but strictly regulated separation of the activities of each person. It cares a good deal about means and little about ends. Instead of defining objectives precisely, and leaving to those who carry them out the greatest latitude in the choice of methods, it details the methods without deciding upon the long-range objectives.

Jean-Jacques Servan-Schreiber, *The American Challenge* (New York: Atheneum, 1968), pp. 251–8.

DOCUMENT 13   THE STUDENT UPRISING OF MAY 1968

The following leaflet, written at the beginning of the struggle in the Latin Quarter, describes the battles between police and students at the Sorbonne, and calls upon its readers to join a general strike in protest.

Halt Repression!

For the first time in the history of the University, the Sorbonne has been invaded by police, to prevent the meeting for solidarity with the Nanterre students organised by the National Union of French Students [UNEF]. 'Although no incident had occurred during the meeting' ... nearly 600 students were arrested.

The riot police came inside the Sorbonne and forced the demonstrators to evacuate the premises in small groups which were directed toward Black Marias.

Students who happened to be outside the Sorbonne protesting against this deliberate violation of the fundamental right of assembly, spontaneously demonstrated throughout the Latin Quarter, where they were chased and brutally hit by the riot police and the so-called 'guardians of peace.'

The national guard were leading the fight. They even charged into the halls of apartment houses, invaded several hotels and came out with young people whom they beat up while the public booed. Because of the general reprobation, they stopped, but one of them was heard to say to another, 'You won't lose anything by waiting. ... '

The police reaction reached its climax when the order was given to 'clear everything': Blackjacks held high, the national guard attacked, hitting with all their might in all directions. Old women were caught in the general turmoil. A passing motorist shouted his indignation, national guardsmen swooped down on his car and tried to pull him out of it, hitting him while he was still seated. They succeeded at last in getting him out of the vehicle, his face bloodied. ...

This brutal repression has been in the making for several weeks, the result of a systematic campaign of intoxication and calls for police intervention via the press, the radio, and the television. The student movement is presented as being the action of a 'minority of *enragés.*'

Rector Roche: 'a small group of students.'

Dean Grappin: 'the excesses of a few.'

Minister Peyrefitte: 'a handful of trouble makers. ... '

On May 3, 1967, Paris students provided proof that the struggle is not just the affair of a minority. Their spontaneous demonstration brought out more than 2,000 students.

Reform and Blackjacks

The Government has shown, through the use of blackjacks, that it will not stop at any means in order *to liquidate the student movement* before the examination period, when its plan to eliminate hundreds of thousands of us will be implemented.

After the closing of Nanterre ... the blackjacking in the Latin Quarter, the closing of the Sorbonne, the forbidding of the UNEF Paris demonstration on Monday, May 6, *how far will the government go* to muzzle the students and liquidate their union movement? How repressive will M. Fouchet, Minister of the Interior, become, in order to have 'his' reforms applied?

Students, we should not let ourselves be intimidated by repression and threats! ...

Students, we must organise a rebuttal, we must defend our organisation, the UNEF!

SOLIDARITY

With our jailed comrades!
With our comrades who are fighting to protect freedom to unionise!

NO

To police repression!
To mass elimination!

The National Union of Higher Education [FEN], *'in solidarity with the students, calls on the faculty in higher education to strike, in all universities.'*

The UNEF calls on all students to join the

GENERAL STRIKE
MONDAY, MAY 6, 1968

General Association of Clermont Students, UNEF, leaflet of 5 May 1968, reproduced in Alain Schnapp and Pierre Vidal-Naquet, *The French Student Uprising, November 1967–June 1968: an Analytical Documentary* (Boston, MA: Beacon, 1971), pp. 156–8.

DOCUMENT 14   **THE ESTABLISHED LEFT RESPONDS TO THE STUDENT REVOLUTIONARIES OF MAY 1968**

At a national council meeting in June 1968 the Communist-controlled General Confederation of Labour (CGT) reaffirmed its support for the reform of higher education, yet at the same time maintained its hostility towards the revolutionary New Left of May.

The events that have occurred among students, and more generally in the university world, have revealed to us the depths of opposition there to Gaullist university policy, and the eagerness of demands for the democratic and modern reform of teaching, demands which figure into the programme of the CGT along with questions of professional training as one of our fundamental objectives.

Thus, here as well, the effects of monopoly domination, the sombre future it offers to manual and intellectual workers, to working-class and student youth, have engendered a reaction against Gaullist power.

From this point of view, taking into account our own action in favour of the reform of teaching and professional training, there exists between students, teachers and workers an objective solidarity, a class solidarity to the extent that it prompts common action against the degrading power of Big Capital.

Nonetheless, while in most provincial university cities things generally went well between workers and students, the common expression of this solidarity was not what it could have been in Paris, where the New Left succeeded in influencing the leadership of the UNEF and the SNE-Sup [Union of Teachers in Higher Education], to the point that some of their representatives tried to impose their anarchist theories, adventurist ideas and provocative slogans upon us, with the goal of taking over the leadership of the movement in order to lead it into a disastrous adventure.

Having always taken care to distinguish these elements from the mass of students ... we have rejected as firmly as possible the activities of these New Left groups which have been clearly shown to have been, at the moment of victory, as the principal supporters of corporate and government strategies.

We sincerely regret the fact that the directors of the UNEF, more exactly some of them, have in effect offered hospitality and a forum in the heart of the students' union to all the New Leftists in France, anarchists, Trotskyites, pro-Chinese and other troublemakers, people whom it is absolutely indispensable to combat.

The evil they have done among students is serious, but we know that conditions are improving and the day is approaching when the CGT and the UNEF will be able to pursue, in the context of mutual respect and independence ... their fertile cooperation for the benefit of workers, of students, and more generally, of democracy.

La Vie Ouvrière, 19 June 1968, p. 43.

DOCUMENT 15   FRENCH INTELLECTUALS REJECT THE LEFT

In 1977 the young philosopher Bernard-Henri Lévy, himself a veteran of the May 1968 student movement, announced his recantation of the Left in a book that condemned not only Marxism but the very idea of progress.

I have said that socialism is in many respects a sham and a deception: When it promises, it lies; when it interprets, it is wrong; it is not and cannot be the alternative it says it is. But in addition, through its very mistakes, it also produces concrete effects. Although it is incapable of bringing happiness to men, it can very well, by desperately attempting to make them believe it possible, bring them misery. It is not only a trap, but that trap can become a catastrophe. I will not repeat the usual qualifications. I will simply note that if we take its discourse literally and grasp the root of its activities, it, too, does nothing but articulate and embody, with the greatest seriousness, the dream of capital. It is, paradoxically, socialism that thinks it through and formulates it. Socialism names the unnamable and gives it an ontological foundation. In other words, while the bourgeoisie retreats and hesitates before the horror, socialism cheerfully depicts it, makes out of it the colours of its palette, and even the colours of its future.

Everyone knows, for example, that the classless society is in a certain sense the practical embodiment of the totalitarian dream of the advent of the universal; that a Marxist politics is very often nothing but the promise of that transparency of the self and that ultimate reconciliation which, by reducing the distance between reality and language, condemns the world to unity, amorphousness, and equivalence; that Marxist theory itself, because it sanctifies the Hegelian dream of the truth becoming the world and the world becoming the truth, ends up with an ideal which is, as we shall see, one of the definitions of modern tyranny. If it is true that capital is the conclusion of the West, then Stalinism is the conclusion of that conclusion. If it is true that the first is the waning of a decadence, then the second is the decadence of that waning. What is the Gulag? The Enlightenment minus tolerance. What is the five-year plan? Bourgeois economism plus police and terror. Socialism in power is the knowledge of bourgeois illusions; socialism in operation is an absent-mindedness of capital. ...

What is social equality for a socialist but the political result of a growth of *productive forces* which the most diabolical capitalists never dared dream of? What is the reversal of Hegelianism for a Marxist but the substitution of man the master of technology for spirit the master of the absolute? It is as though, to the old question of *being*, socialism answered with an apology for *work*; as if, to the question of revolution, it answered first of all with an extraordinary display of tools and machines. Marx is not only the thinker of technology; he is also, even especially, the thinker of the factory, the only one who dared to investigate its darkest aspects. It is not enough to mention his fascination with the industrial revolution and the bourgeoisie of his time; we have to go further and say that he imagines the new world only as their truth and their most complete representation. In other words, socialism in power is not only a form of capital; it is a *barbarian* form which is afraid of no shortcut, no historical short-circuit, in order to lead societies to the sterility that capital promised them.

Technology, desire, and socialism: these are the three primary faces of the contemporary tragedy. They are the three dangers threatening the future of the West. Beware totalitarianism with a technocratic, a sexual, or a revolutionary face. Parodying Nietzsche, I am willing to assert that a century of barbarism is approaching and they will be at its service.

Bernard-Henri Lévy, *Barbarism with a Human Face* (New York: Harper and Row, 1979), pp. 118–21.

DOCUMENT 16   THE SOCIALIST VICTORY OF 1981

On the night of 10 May 1981, after learning of his party's decisive victory and his election as the new president of France, François Mitterrand made the following speech at a press conference.

This victory belongs to the forces of youth, of labour, of creativity, of renewal who have come together in a great national movement for jobs, peace, freedom, themes which were those of my presidential campaign and will remain those of my administration.

It is also a victory of these women, of these men, humble activists fired with idealism who, in every community in France, in every city, every village, all their lives, have hoped for the day when their country would finally take cognisance of their efforts.

To all I owe both the honour and the responsibility for the duties which I will henceforth bear. I will not distinguish between them. They are our people, and nothing else. I have no other ambition than to justify their confidence.

In this instant my thoughts go out towards those family and friends, no longer with us, who gave me the simple love for my country and the will to serve without fail. I measure the weight of History, its rigour, its grandeur. Only the entire national community should respond to the demands of the present day. ... We have so much to do together, and so much to say as well.

Hundreds of millions of people throughout the world will know tonight that France is ready to speak to them in the language that they have learned to expect from her, and to love.

I have one more brief declaration to make. To M. Giscard d'Estaing who I thank for his message, I address the thanks that I owe to the man who, for seven years, has led France. Beyond political struggles and contradictions, it is History that now has the responsibility of judging our acts.

François Mitterrand, *Politique, 1977–1981* (Paris: Fayard, 1982), p. 299.

DOCUMENT 17   THE RISE OF THE NATIONAL FRONT

In 1983 voters in the city of Dreux, near Paris, gave the National Front one of its first major victories, awarding it control of the city council. In this excerpt, Françoise Gaspard, the city's Socialist mayor at the time, describes the rise of the far Right in local politics.

Less than a year after Mitterrand's election to the presidency and the Socialist Party's capture of an absolute majority in parliament, the political climate had turned against the left. The 'state of grace,' as Mitterrand's honeymoon period was dubbed by the French press, was long since over. What had revived the opposition was none other than the immigrant question, and in particular the foreign minister's mention, during a visit to Algiers, of the possibility of granting foreigners the right to vote in municipal elections. Meanwhile, tensions in Dreux were growing. Copies of a letter allegedly written by an Algerian living in France to a friend back home had been circulating since the summer of 1981. The text read in part: 'Dear Mustapha. By the grace of all-powerful Allah we have become the lords and masters of Paris. I wonder why you hesitate to join us.' Mustapha's friend goes on to enumerate all the benefits that France holds in store for him, his children, and his women and then closes with a flourish: 'So you see that your presence here is indispensable, and who knows if you might not be elected to the future council of *émigrés*. Come soon. Lots of us await your arrival, because Mitterrand has promised to grant us the right to vote very soon now. We kicked the French out of Algeria. Why shouldn't we do the same thing here?' ... This was in late July 1981.

Starting with this campaign, Dreux would serve as a testing site for various forms of racist, anti-Arab propaganda. The tests were appalling but effective. Eighteen months later, this same letter would be circulated throughout France during the 1983 legislative election campaign. It became so well known, in fact, that Patrick Jarreau wrote an article printed on the front page of *Le Monde* under the title 'Dear Mustapha.' ... When a pamphlet containing one such purported letter was posted on the bulletin board of a small company outside Paris, an immigrant worker went to the plant manager to protest, only to be told that 'it's just a political flyer.'

Who initiated the Mustapha letter? Nobody knows. It appears to have surfaced first in Dreux, which, given the composition of its population and the presence of the xenophobic virus, was an ideal proving ground. At the time, the extreme right had no headquarters in the city and only two or three known activists. The National Front's office was no more than a mail drop, actually a post-office box rented by a plant manager who led a quiet life out of the public eye. Given his past, it is easy to understand why he shunned publicity: he had been a participant in Vichy's Chantiers de Jeunesse (Youth Works Projects) and had served as a group leader in charge of training recruits to the Militia (*la Milice*), the paramilitary collaborationist organisation that provided the Vichy regime's muscle. After the Liberation he fled, probably to Spain. Resistance fighters from the Lot-et-Garonne who survived the Militia's punitive searches and strong-arm interrogations still remember him. He was sentenced, in absentia, to death for treason, armed combat against France, and intelligence with the enemy. In 1952, after French war criminals were amnestied, he surfaced and was arrested for flight to avoid prosecution in 1945. In 1953 he was sentenced to five years at hard labor. A few months later the sentence was suspended. ...

In the [1982 cantonal election] campaign the two Stirbois [Jean-Pierre and Marie, leaders of the local National Front] appealed to different groups. He courted the working-class vote by once again denouncing the Communist Party's alleged collusion with immigrants against the interests of French workers, while she issued position papers denouncing the so-called *taxe professionnelle* in a move designed to attract the votes of merchants and professionals. She also issued a warning against the 'Marxization of teaching' in the public schools in an appeal for the family vote. Last but not least, both cantons were flooded with brochures blaming the invasion of France by 'hordes of immigrants' on the parties of both the right and the left. ...

That 1983 municipal election campaign was strange indeed. Rumors flew: it was said that 800 new Turkish workers would soon arrive in the city; that the mayor was having a factory built to employ them; that the mayor had arranged for the release of the murderer of a shopping-mall security guard and had offered him a job at city hall; that the mayor would authorise the building of a mosque at Les Chamards; last but not least, that the mayor had secretly had a child by a Moroccan man and was keeping the child hidden. In addition to these wild rumors, which were not too different from those circulating at the same time in places like Roubaix, Grenoble, and Chambéry, a new form of propaganda was tried for the first time. Here is a report that appeared in *Le Nouvel Observateur* on 4 March 1983: 'Over the past few days a strange group of political campaigners has descended on the Prod'hommes section of Dreux, the poorest neighbourhood in the city. These energetic spokesmen pass themselves off as salesmen and go from door to door in the projects. Their sample cases are filled with various items, all of them expensive: VCRs, hi-fi systems, jewelry. When the door opens, they greet the lady of the house: "Good day, madam. Are you interested? No? Too bad! Your neighbor (Mohammed or Miloud or Youssef) has two of them. I'm not kidding you. Thanks to Madame Gaspard, the Arabs around here earn more than the French."'

The Jean-Pierre Stirbois of 1983 was no longer the street fighter of 1979. The *Nouvel Observateur* article continued: 'Friday, 11 February, 8:30 p.m. Big public rally on behalf of the RPR-National Front. Where are the combat fatigues, the leather jackets, the muscles, and all the paraphernalia of old? There were no more than five shaved heads in the back of the room. At the National Front convention [in 1982] Stirbois had shouted, "Immigrants from across the Mediterranean, back to your shacks!"' At this rally Stirbois, looking like a banker in polished shoes and smart trousers, expressed himself more soberly: "The people of Dreux will defend their historical and cultural identity. ... The flow of immigration must be reversed."'

Françoise Gaspard, *A Small City in France* (Cambridge, MA: Harvard University Press, 1995), pp. 117–19, 123–4.

DOCUMENT 18   THE LAY PUBLIC SCHOOL AND THE ISLAMIC VEIL

In the following excerpt Elizabeth Altschull, lycée professor and committed progressive, recounts her conflicts with a young student who insisted upon wearing an Islamic headscarf in her school.

In September 1992, having taught in Paris, I began a new year in a school in the suburbs north of Paris. The opening of the year passed without problem. Two weeks later, Aïcha, 13 years old, comes to my eighth grade class in history and geography wearing a veil. My immediate reaction is to tell her to remove it in the name of secular education, to respect the principle of religious neutrality. I pose my demand calmly, much more so than my request to a young man to take off his backward baseball cap and his noisy Walkman. In fact, my reflex is more feminist than secular, strictly speaking: to veil such a young girl seems clearly unacceptable to me. If I certainly see the spark of defiance in her eyes, I do not suspect to what point this defiance will be untiringly supported by her parents. The psychosis that will become evident among many teachers is even less foreseeable. After all, it's our job to rule adolescent defiance.

I refuse to start class as long as Aïcha continues to wear her headscarf. She gives up after a few minutes, and the class is henceforth very quiet. The same day, I meet with the headmaster of this school ... to inform him of the incident. He is clearly not enchanted at the prospect of having been 'parachuted' into a school where 'the headscarf problem' exists (he has just been transferred to this thankless suburban position), and is a bit angry with me for not having 'let this pass calmly'. However, being of socialist sympathies, and before my affirmation of my secular convictions, he adopts the following position: every professor is sovereign in his own class as far as the wearing of veils is concerned. He announces a few days later, during a meeting of the school's teaching staff, that he will support those who wish their students to take off their headscarves during class.

The result of this is an awkward compromise; Aïcha keeps her veil on in the schoolyard, in the hallways, and in the classes of those teachers too timid to demand firmly its removal. In my class, she always keeps her headscarf on at the beginning of class, until I reiterate the request to take it off, having from all accounts begun a war of attrition. Disturbed to find myself isolated, and having the impression that Aïcha has not been given a clear message, I contact the local branch of the SNES (National Union of Secondary School Teachers), which gives me its firm support. During the next few days I try to begin a discussion little by little with my colleagues, the majority of whom oppose the wearing of the veil in school. From very different perspectives, from the practising Catholic who is nonetheless attached to secularism, to the committed New Left activist, and with many different positions in between, those opposed to the wearing of the veil form a discrete, heterogeneous, and hesitant majority.

One lone colleague takes an aggressive posture towards me, suggesting that I am intolerant or a natural troublemaker. ... Thus, for the first time in my life, it is insinuated that my last name could play some role in deciding my opinions. A modern woman, this colleague and English teacher, of Kabyle origin who does not wear the veil, tries to create with the other North African colleagues (in the school lunchroom, around the coffee machine) an agreement about the ambient 'racism' of the 'others'. During one of our confrontations she recognised that I am 'doubtless less in-different than the others' and that I care 'more than those who don't think about the issue at all, or who don't care about it anyway'. This is the most striking example, but not the only one, of this strange gift which the presence of one young veiled girl had ... to turn professors against each other, and to make everyone suspicious.

My strongest support definitely comes from the superintendents, almost all of Muslim origin; their support is active in deed and enlightening in discussion. The professors of Arabic, or of North African origin, are very discrete; they do not favour the veil but don't speak out frankly against it. My most trying experience in this affair is a discourse which takes place here and there between my colleagues. Thus, one can hear people say, in the school lunchroom or in the professors' lounge, that Muslims are 'different', that they can get married 'through marriages arranged at the age of 16 and be happy'. I have the feeling of having fallen into a sort of nightmare, where the world is turned upside down, where nothing makes any sense, where the customary references and values are, for some unknown reason, abandoned by those around me.

Elizabeth Altschull, *Le voile contre l'école* (Paris: Editions du Seuil, 1995), pp. 11–13.

DOCUMENT 19   FRANCE WINS THE WORLD CUP

The French victory in the 1998 World Cup, won by a team led by an Algerian and including members of Caribbean, Armenian, Ghanaian, Italian, Pacific islander, Basque and Breton origin, symbolised a new day for national unity and identity. The Le Monde *article excerpted below reports on the wild celebrations that greeted this soccer triumph.*

On the pavement of the Champs Elysées, Zora, a forty-year-old pharmacist, can't stop crying while looking at the smiling crowd. On the Arch of Triumph the words 'thanks a million Zidane' [the team leader] flash on and off in luminous letters. One man, without speaking, puts his hand under the nose of another and signals 'one, two, three' with his fingers. 'Everyone sit down'. And old people, youth, women, and children burst into laughter, squatting on the pavement, and wait thirty seconds. Twenty times, one hundred times, they jump into the air. Roland, 60 years old, speaks to Ibrahim, 25, in a streetwise Parisian accent: 'You are black. The first time I saw a black person was during the Liberation, with the Americans. My daughter is married to an Indonesian, that's the way life is these days.' Ibrahim: 'France loses when she discriminates. Here, we were forced to win, forced.'

Roland looks in his wallet for his photos of the Liberation, not finding them. 'I haven't seen so many people since the Liberation,' he remarks. Zora is still crying. Her neighbour, Nathalie, thirty years old, machinist, says 'It's too beautiful, too beautiful, it is the awakening of France.' Zora searches for words: 'We should always be doing good things like this. Look, there are no more barriers between us. We should have a World Cup every year, every day,' she sobs.

Since the beginning of the afternoon Paris has been drunk with victory. 'Awaken, the people must awaken' shouts Laurent, his torso a gaudy pastiche of red white and blue. He stole the huge Tricolour flag from in front of the city hall of the little town in the Aude where he lives. A car passes by, one of its passengers sticking his head out the window to blow a trumpet. Laurent yells at Karim: 'Don't step on my flag!'. Karim: 'Oh, you have an accent, where are you from?' 'Marseilles', responds Laurent with the wink of an eye, saying, 'These Parisians...'

The evening of the semi-finals Laurent said to himself 'I've got to get to Paris immediately'. So did Manuel, the truck driver from Haute Saône who drives to Rungis [in the Paris suburbs] several times a week. Like Marie, a promoter from Fontenay-sous-Bois (Val de Marne), who rejoices to see the posters showing the face of Le Pen and a photograph of the soccer stadium, saying 'We have put hate in the cupboard.'

Nobody can move anymore in front of the Paris City Hall. Teenagers climb on the roofs, on the gutters, some hang suspended from the lampposts. 'Blacks, Arabs, you will have your victory tonight', shouts a young man. 'Give them papers!', an unknown person in the crowd responds. Coloured searchlights have been turned on, lifting the edges of the fog. Léandre, twenty five years old, gazes at all the flags, all the people made up in the colours of France, and says: 'They say that the people have come out in the same way that they used to for wars. Perhaps soccer has replaced war now. However, one still wonders if it might not degenerate.' Fatima points, places her finger on three little red white and blue stripes that Freddy, an African, has painted on his shirt: 'Wow, you've been kissed', she kids him. Far from the giant projection screen, stuck in a little side street, Estelle, twenty four years old, sings the Marseillaise at the top of her lungs: '*the bloody standard is raised*; this is a communion', she announces, 'a type of Utopia'.

Le Monde, 14 July 1998, p. xvi.

GLOSSARY

Algeria A nation in North Africa that was a French colony from 1830 to 1962. From 1954 to 1962 it witnessed a bitter colonial war between Algerian freedom fighters and French forces, one featuring widespread torture and brutality committed by both sides against soldiers and civilians alike. France conceded Algerian independence in 1962.

Enragés 'The enraged ones'. The student movement that originated at the Nanterre campus of the University of Paris in 1967 and led the student uprising of May 1968. The *enragés* rejected contemporary French society as both oppressive and soulless, criticising not only capitalism but the traditional French Left as well. Notable leaders included Daniel Cohn-Bendit and Alain Krivine.

Existentialism A political and cultural philosophy that became popular among French intellectuals during the years after the Second World War. Its main tenets included a belief that human existence was in many ways tragic, yet distinguished by an imperative to strive for freedom. It strongly emphasised the importance of political activism for intellectuals. Jean-Paul Sartre was generally recognised as the leader of the movement.

Fifth Republic The French regime that has lasted from 1958 to the present day. Largely constructed by Charles de Gaulle, its first president until his resignation in 1969, the Fifth Republic has emphasised a strong executive branch. Its president is elected for a seven-year term. The other major figure of the Fifth Republic has been François Mitterrand, who served as president from 1981 to 1995.

Fourth Republic The French regime that followed the Second World War, lasting from 1946 to 1958. The Fourth Republic was characterised by a series of weak governments that often proved inadequate when faced with major crises, especially those involving the empire. At the same time, however, the Fourth Republic presided over the beginnings of a period of unprecedented prosperity for France.

French Communist Party (PCF) Founded in 1920, the PCF is the official Communist party of France, and for much of the postwar era was one of the biggest Communist parties in the non-Communist world. A leading French political party, it traditionally won much of the working-class vote and had a strong presence in labour unions. Starting in the late 1970s it began to decline in importance.

French Socialist Party (SFIO, PS) Founded in 1906, during the postwar years the Socialists represented the moderate left wing in French politics, one that appealed to many workers and intellectuals, in particular teachers. Its vision of socialism emphasised welfare state benefits and democracy, not violent revolution. Part of many governing coalitions under the Fourth Republic, it was isolated during de Gaulle's presidency. In 1971 François Mitterrand refounded the party at its Epinay conference, changing its initials from SFIO to PS, and giving it a new dynamism. This made it the dominant political party in France after 1980.

General Confederation of Labour (CGT)   The main trade union organisation in France. Since the immediate postwar period the CGT has been effectively controlled by the Communist Party. The end of postwar prosperity and the decline of the traditional working class in France has dented its power since the 1970s.

Indochina   France's colony in Southeast Asia, consisting of what are today the nations of Vietnam, Cambodia and Laos. A French colony since the 1880s, Indochina became the site of a major war of independence from French rule from 1946 to 1954. After a catastrophic defeat by Vietnamese independence forces at Dien Bien Phu, Paris admitted defeat and French rule came to an end.

Liberation   The freeing of France from Nazi occupation and Vichy rule at the end of the Second World War. Paris was liberated on 25 August 1944, and the Germans ousted from all of French soil by the spring of 1945. For many French, the Liberation represented not only a military victory but a hoped-for political and spiritual renewal of French society.

Marshall Plan   This was an extensive programme of economic aid proposed by the American government in 1947 to help European nations recover from the ravages of the Second World War. The aid came with strings attached for France, including participation in European integration and support for West German rearmament. Most importantly, France's acceptance of Marshall Plan aid led to the expulsion of the PCF from the government and the nation's siding with the United States during the Cold War. Ultimately, France received billions of dollars in Marshall Plan aid, which made a major contribution to its postwar recovery.

National Liberation Front (FLN)   The FLN was the main organisation of Algerian freedom fighters, which led the nation to independence from France during the Algerian war. Enjoying widespread popular support but military weakness, it engaged in widespread torture against French soldiers and civilians (as well as Algerians opposed to its ideas), and ultimately succeeded in rendering continued French rule militarily and politically untenable.

Planning   Starting in 1947 France initiated a series of Five Year Plans to organise and facilitate the recovery and modernisation of the French economy. This kind of planning represented a compromise between capitalism and socialism, and also had deep roots in the French tradition of centralisation. Emphasising government coordination of industrial efforts through programmes of targets and incentives, planning deserves a large share of the credit for the nation's postwar economic success.

The Resistance   During the Occupation a small number of French women and men engaged in organised resistance against the German Occupation and the Vichy state. In general the Resistance hoped not just to end German rule, but also to create a new, more equitable French society after the war. Led by Charles de Gaulle and with the heavy participation of the PCF, after the war the Resistance inherited the moral leadership of the nation, if not always concrete political control.

Structuralism   This was a philosophy that became prominent in France during the 1960s, constituting the major intellectual successor to existentialism. Structuralists stressed that human life was governed primarily by a series of cognitive and institutional structures, so that individuals had relatively little autonomy or freedom to shape their own lives. Some of its major representatives included the anthropologist Claude Lévi-Strauss, the literary critic Roland Barthes, and the psychologist Jacques Lacan.

Third Republic The longest of regimes in modern France, the Third Republic lasted from 1870 to France's defeat by Nazi Germany in 1940. In its later years the governments of the Third Republic were often seen as weak and ineffectual, so that many members of the Resistance hoped to see it replaced with a more dynamic regime. In actual fact, however, the Fourth Republic bore a striking similarity to its predecessor in many respects.

Trente Glorieuses This was the period of economic growth and prosperity in France that lasted roughly thirty years, from the late 1940s to the mid-1970s. During this period the French population grew sharply, and the general population was able to enjoy an unprecedented level of consumer comforts. This period also transformed French society, creating the France that we know today.

Tripartism This was a short-lived coalition between the PCF, the SFIO and the MRP that ruled France for a few months in 1946–47. Tripartism represented an attempt to maintain the unity of the Resistance coalition after the war, and to avoid taking sides in the Cold War. Tripartism collapsed in April 1947, when France opted for Marshall Plan aid and the Communists left the government.

Vichy This was the collaborationist regime set up by the French during the German Occupation of the Second World War. Representing both a desire to collaborate with Nazi Germany and long-standing right-wing traditions in French politics, Vichy pursued its own anti-Semitic policies and waged war against the forces of the French Resistance. It collapsed with the German withdrawal in 1944.

Viet Minh This was the guerrilla army of the Indochinese Communist Party, headed by Communist leader Ho Chi Minh. Formed in 1941 in response to the Japanese invasion of Indochina, the Viet Minh demanded national independence from both Japan and France. It led the successful military effort against the French, winning independence for the nations of Indochina in 1954.

WHO'S WHO

Aron, Raymond (1905–83)   A major Left Bank philosopher and intellectual of the postwar years. Although a good friend of Sartre, Aron rejected his emphasis on left-wing political activism, preferring Anglo-American liberalism. In 1955 he published *The Opium of the Intellectuals*, a major attack on France's Marxist intellectuals. He also disagreed strongly with the student radicals of May 1968.

de Beauvoir, Simone (1908–86)   De Beauvoir was one of the leading postwar existentialist philosophers and the life-long companion of Jean-Paul Sartre. She was also one of France's most prominent feminist intellectuals. Her 1949 book, *The Second Sex*, inspired a generation of French women to demand gender equality and the end of patriarchy.

Camus, Albert (1913–60)   One of the greatest novelists of twentieth-century France, and a winner of the Nobel Prize for Literature, Camus also played a major part in the Left Bank after the Liberation. Born in Algeria, he had a prominent role in the Resistance. By the 1950s he had shifted towards a more moderate political position, feuding publicly with Sartre about the role of intellectuals in politics. He died tragically in a Paris car crash in 1960.

Chirac, Jacques (1932–)   The President of France since 1995, and leader of the Gaullist party. From a rural middle-class background, and a veteran of the Algerian war, Chirac was elected to parliament and became the youngest minister in Pompidou's government in 1967. Elected mayor of Paris in 1977, Chirac then became prime minister under Mitterrand during the 'cohabitation' period of 1986–88, and the effective leader of the Gaullist party.

Cohn-Bendit, Daniel (1945–)   The charismatic leader of the student revolutionaries in Nanterre, Cohn-Bendit, more than anyone else, symbolised the revolt of May 1968. A German national, he returned to West Germany after 1968 and gradually became involved in the politics of the Green Party. In 1999 he was elected to the European Parliament as a representative of the French Green Party.

Foucault, Michel (1926–84)   One of the most important Parisian philosophers of the period after 1968, Foucault was a major pioneer of post-structuralist philosophy. In his works, like *Discipline and Punish* and *The Archaeology of Knowledge*, Foucault explored issues of power and marginality in modern societies. His later work also reflected the increasing conservatism of French intellectuals in the 1970s and 1980s.

de Gaulle, Charles (1890–1970)   The leader of Free French forces during the Second World War, and the founder of the Fifth Republic, de Gaulle was unquestionably the single most important individual in the history of postwar France. After retreating to private life following the failure of the Fourth Republic to meet his desires for strong leadership, de Gaulle returned to power during the Algerian crisis of 1958. He served ten years as president of France, presiding over decolonisation and economic expansion, before resigning in 1969.

Giscard-d'Estaing, Valéry (1926–)   Giscard-d'Estaing served as president of France from 1974 to 1981, representing the UDF, a centre-right political party. Of an aristocratic and technocratic background, Giscard-d'Estaing came to power determined to complete the modernisation of French society. However, the international economic crisis of the 1970s short-circuited these hopes, and he was defeated by François Mitterrand in 1981.

Godard, Jean-Luc (1930–)   One of the leading filmmakers in France, and a prominent representative of the New Wave school of French films. A pioneer of innovative cinematic techniques, Godard also used films like *Weekend* and *Alphaville* to chronicle and critique changes in French society. Although his films since the late 1960s have generally not lived up to the quality of his earlier work, he remains active today.

Ho Chi Minh (1890?–1969)   Born in French Indochina, Ho Chi Minh became the leader of the Indochinese Communist Party and the mastermind behind Vietnam's successful revolt against French rule. After 1954 he became the head of Communist North Vietnam, dying in 1969 during his nation's war with the United States. Vietnam finally achieved full unity and independence in 1975.

Lang, Jack (1939–)   During the 1980s Lang achieved fame, and notoriety, as the Mitterrand administration's youthful minister of culture. A dynamic individual full of ideas about promoting French culture, he emphasised democratising artistic and creative life in France. Some of his efforts included extending government subsidies to museums and libraries throughout the country, and founding a National Music Day in 1982.

Le Pen, Jean-Marie (1928–)   Le Pen is one of the founders, and the most important leader, of the National Front, a right-wing extremist party which has made a name for itself in the 1980s and 1990s by denouncing immigrants and adopting racist positions. Le Pen fought in colonial wars in both Indochina and Algeria, and was a follower of the neo-fascist leader Pierre Poujade during the 1950s. Even after the 1999 split in the National Front, Le Pen remains its leader and one of the most noteworthy and powerful politicians in France.

Mitterrand, François (1916–96)   Mitterrand was one of the most prominent political leaders in postwar France, second only to de Gaulle in importance. He took over the leadership of the Socialist Party in 1971, enabling it to compete more effectively with the PCF anwd take over the leadership of the French Left. In 1981 he was elected president of France, a position he held for fourteen years. Under his leadership the Socialists have become arguably the strongest political party in contemporary France.

Monnet, Jean (1888–1979)   A brandy merchant and the only prominent business-man to join de Gaulle in exile during the Second World War, after the war Monnet pioneered France's efforts at centralised economic planning. He served as the director of the National Planning Commission and orchestrated the first Five Year Plan. Monnet thus played a central role in the postwar modernisation of the French economy.

Sartre, Jean-Paul (1905–80)   Arguably the most prominent intellectual in postwar France, Jean-Paul Sartre is most closely associated with the philosophy of existentialism and the intelligentsia of the Left Bank in the 1940s and 1950s. Founder of the leading journal *Les Temps Modernes*, Sartre always believed that intellectuals had a duty to take political positions, and he frequently voiced his support for the Left, both in France and around the world.

REFERENCES

Ardagh, John, *France in the New Century.* London: Penguin, 1999.

Berstein, Serge, *The Republic of De Gaulle, 1958–1969.* Cambridge: Cambridge University Press, 1993.

Fenby, Jonathan, *France on the Brink: A Great Civilization Faces the New Century.* New York: Arcade Publishing, 1999.

Flanner, Janet, *Paris Journal, 1944–1955.* New York: Harcourt Brace and Co., 1965.

Gildea, Robert, *France since 1945.* Oxford/New York: Oxford University Press, 1996.

Kuisel, Richard, *Seducing the French: the dilemma of Americanisation.* Berkeley, CA: University of California Press, 1993.

Lottman, Herbert, *The Left Bank.* San Francisco, CA: Halo Books, 1991.

New York Times, 18 March 1992.

Paxton, Robert, *Vichy France: Old Guard and New Order.* New York: Columbia University Press, 1972.

Rioux, Jean-Pierre, *The Fourth Republic, 1944–1958.* Cambridge: Cambridge University Press, 1987.

Werth, Alexander, *France 1940–1945.* Boston, MA: Beacon Press, 1956.

GUIDE TO FURTHER READING

One of the benefits of the study of contemporary history is plentiful sources. The student wishing to investigate the history of France in the last half of the twentieth century is fortunate in having a wide variety of writings at her or his disposal. Although the large majority of texts on the subject are, of course, written in French, many have been translated into English, giving Anglophone readers a broad range of choices. The following guide is intended to introduce readers to some of the more useful texts in contemporary French history.

One can choose from a wide array of primary sources, texts written by individuals who either took part directly in this history, or else lived at the time it occurred. Since some of the individuals discussed in this book are still alive or have only recently passed on, the reader has several choices. Alexander Werth, *France 1940–1945* (Boston, MA: Beacon Press, 1956) provides an insightful political and social commentary on the ten years after the war. Janet Flanner wrote a series of 'Letters from Paris' to the *New Yorker* magazine for nearly fifty years; her three-volume *Paris Journal: 1944–55; 1956–64;1965–70* (New York: Harcourt Brace Co., 1965) provides a lively, informal discussion of the life of the French capital. Memoirs and other books by politicians themselves constitute a valuable source. See Charles de Gaulle, *Memoirs of Hope: Renewal and Endeavour* (New York: Simon and Schuster, 1971); Valéry Giscard-d'Estaing, *Towards a New Democracy* (London: Collins, 1977); François Mitterrand, *The Wheat and the Chaff* (New York: Seaver Books, 1982); Mitterrand and Elie Wiesel, *A Memoir in Two Voices* (New York: Arcade, 1996). Daniel Cohn-Bendit's *Obsolete Communism: The Left-Wing Alternative* (New York: McGraw Hill, 1968) shows the ideals of the May 1968 movement from the perspective of its most important leader. Simone de Beauvoir's *The Mandarins* (Cleveland, OH: World Publishing Co., 1956) provides a lively, personal look at the world of Left Bank intellectuals immediately after the Liberation. Régis Debray gives an overview of the world of French intellectuals in *Teachers, Writers, Celebrities. The Intellectuals of Modern France* (London: New Left Books, 1981). Laurence Wylie's *Village in the Vaucluse* (Cambridge, MA: Harvard University Press, 1957) gives an intimate glimpse of life in a French village during the 1950s. Jean-Jacques Servan-Schreiber, *Lieutenant in Algeria* (New York: Alfred Knopf, 1957) is a revealing memoir about the French Army in the Algerian war. Frantz Fanon, *The Wretched of the Earth* (New York: Grove Press, 1963) is an interesting comment on Algeria and colonialism in general by a noted black French intellectual.

Useful general studies of this period include Robert Gildea, *France since 1945* (Oxford/New York: Oxford University Press, 1996); James F. McMillan, *Twentieth Century France* (London: Edward Arnold, 1992); Maurice Larkin, *France since the Popular Front* (Oxford: Clarendon Press, 1986). Olivier Wieviorka and Christophe Prochasson, *La France du XXe siècle: documents d'histoire* (Paris: Editions du Seuil, 1994) is a fine collection of documents on the history of twentieth-century France.

Also useful are the studies of contemporary France by John Ardagh: *France Today* (London: Penguin, 1990); and *France in the New Century* (London: Penguin, 1999). On the period from the Liberation to the end of Tripartism, see Irwin Wall, *The United States and the Making of Postwar France, 1945–1954* (Cambridge: Cambridge University Press, 1991); Jean-Pierre Rioux, *The Fourth Republic, 1944–1958* (Cambridge: Cambridge University Press, 1987); Richard Vinen, *Bourgeois Politics in France, 1945–1951* (Cambridge: Cambridge University Press, 1995); Philip Williams, *Crisis and Compromise: Politics in the Fourth Republic* (Hamden, CT: Archon Books, 1964); and Bruce D. Graham, *The French Socialists and Tripartism* (Toronto: University of Toronto Press, 1965).

A variety of works deal with the period of French life known as the *trente glorieuses*. On economic growth and prosperity, see J.-J. Carré, et al., *French Economic Growth* (Stanford, CA: Stanford University Press, 1976); Richard Kuisel, *Capitalism and the State in Modern France* (Cambridge: Cambridge University Press, 1981); Serge Berstein, *The Republic of de Gaulle, 1958–1969* (Cambridge: Cambridge University Press, 1993). On social change, consult Gordon Wright, *Rural Revolution in France* (Stanford, CA: Stanford University Press, 1964); Henri Mendras, *Social Change in Modern France* (Cambridge: Cambridge University Press, 1991). Michel Crozier, *The Stalled Society* (New York: Viking, 1973) criticises the continuing rigidities of French society, whereas Luc Boltanski, *The Making of a Class. Cadres in French History* (Cambridge: Cambridge University Press, 1987) considers the rise of the new managerial middle class. On women, see Simone de Beauvoir, *The Second Sex* (London: David Campbell, 1953); Claire Duchen, *Feminism in France from May '68 to Mitterrand* (London: Routledge, 1986); and Claire Laubier, ed., *The Condition of Women in France, 1945 to the Present* (London: Routledge, 1990). On immigration, see Gérard Noiriel, *The French Melting Pot* (Minneapolis, MN: University of Minnesota Press, 1996); and Gary P. Freeman, *Immigrant Labor and Racial Conflict in Industrial Societies: the French and British Experiences, 1945–1975* (Princeton, NJ: Princeton University Press, 1979). In *Seducing the French: the Dilemma of Americanization* (Berkeley, CA: University of California Press, 1993), Richard Kuisel considers French views of American society as a mirror of their own. Among the many biographies of Charles de Gaulle to be recommended are Andrew Shennan, *de Gaulle* (London: Longman, 1993); and Jean Lacouture, *de Gaulle* (New York: Norton, 1990).

There is now a substantial secondary literature in English on the end of the French empire. Good overviews include Raymond Betts, *France and Decolonisation, 1900–1960* (Basingstoke: Macmillan, 1991); Anthony Clayton, *The Wars of French Decolonisation* (London: Longman, 1994); and Miles Kahler, *Decolonization in Britain and France* (Princeton, NJ: Princeton University Press, 1984). For the war in Indochina, see Jacques Dalloz, *The War in Indochina, 1945–1954* (Dublin: Gill and Macmillan, 1990); Bernard Fall, *Street without Joy: Indochina at War 1946–1954* (Harrisburg, PA: Stackpole Co., 1961); R.E.M. Irving, *The First Indo-China War* (London: Croom Helm, 1975). Many accounts exist of the war in Algeria, including Alistair Horne, *A Savage War of Peace* (Basingstoke: Macmillan, 1977); Michael Kettle, *de Gaulle and Algeria, 1940–1960* (London: Quartet Books, 1993). For the decolonisation of black Africa and French relations with former colonies, see Prosser Gifford and William Roger Louis, *The Transfer of Power in Africa: Decolonization, 1940–1960* (New Haven, CT: Yale University Press, 1982); Dorothy

S. White, *Black Africa and de Gaulle: From the French Empire to Independence* (University Park, MD: University of Maryland Press, 1979); John Chipman, *French Power in Africa* (Oxford: Blackwell, 1989); Robert Aldrich and John Connell, eds, *France in World Politics* (London: Routledge, 1989). For a fascinating discussion of the impact of decolonisation on French society, see Kristin Ross, *Fast Cars, Clean Bodies: Decolonization and the Reordering of French Culture* (Cambridge, MA: MIT Press, 1996).

On France's intellectuals, see Jeremy Jennings, *Intellectuals in Twentieth Century France* (Basingstoke: Macmillan, 1993). For the history of the Left Bank during the era of existentialism, see Herbert Lottman, *The Left Bank* (San Francisco, CA: Halo Books, 1991); Tony Judt, *Past Imperfect: French Intellectuals, 1944–1956* (Berkeley, CA: University of California Press, 1992); and Annie Cohen-Solal, *Sartre: A Life* (London: Heinemann, 1987). There are many interesting books about the movement of May 1968, including Alain Touraine, *The May Movement: Revolt and Reform* (New York: Random House, 1971); Daniel Singer, *Prelude to Revolution* (New York: Hill and Wang, 1970); Richard Johnson, *The French Communist Party versus the Students* (New Haven, CT: Yale University Press, 1982). Arthur Hirsh, *The French New Left* (Boston, MA: South End Press, 1981) discusses the intellectual history of the movement. On French intellectuals after 1968, see Keith Reader, *Intellectuals and the Left in France since 1968* (Basingstoke: Macmillan, 1987); Sunil Khilnani, *Arguing Revolution: the Intellectual Left in Postwar France* (New Haven, CT: Yale University Press, 1993); Bernard-Henri Lévy, *Barbarism with a Human Face* (New York: Harper and Row, 1979).

Among the many commentaries on Mitterrand and the Mitterrand era, see Wayne Northcutt, *Mitterrand: a Political Biography* (New York: Holmes and Meier, 1992); Alistair Cole, *Mitterrand: a Study in Political Leadership* (London: Routledge, 1994); Stanley Hoffman, ed., *The Mitterrand Experiment* (Cambridge: Polity Press, 1986); John Laughland, *The Death of Politics: France under Mitterrand* (London: Michael Joseph, 1994); Anthony Daley, ed., *The Mitterrand Era* (New York: New York University Press, 1996). On the economic crisis that began in the 1970s, see John Tuppen, *France under Recession, 1981–1986* (Basingstoke: Macmillan, 1988); John Gaffney, ed., *France and Modernisation* (Aldershot: Avebury, 1988). On memory, Vichy and the Holocaust, see Henry Rousso, *The Vichy Syndrome: History and Memory in France since 1944* (Cambridge, MA: Harvard University Press, 1991). A number of books now deal with the question of immigration and race in contemporary France, including Maxim Silverman, *Deconstructing the Nation: Immigration, Racism and Citizenship in Modern France* (London: Routledge, 1992); Alec Hargreaves, *Immigration, 'Race' and Ethnicity in Contemporary France* (London: Routledge, 1995); Etienne Balibar and Immanuel Wallerstein, *Race, Nation, Class: Ambiguous Identities* (London: Verso, 1991). On the National Front, see Jonathan Marcus, *The National Front and French Politics: the Resistable Rise of Jean-Marie Le Pen* (New York: New York University Press, 1995).

INDEX

Page numbers in *italics* refer to glossary entry.

SEMINAR STUDIES IN HISTORY

General Editors: Clive Emsley & Gordon Martel

The series was founded by Patrick Richardson in 1966. Between 1980 and 1996 Roger Lockyer edited the series before handing over to Clive Emsley (Professor of History at the Open University) and Gordon Martel (Professor of International History at the University of Northern British Columbia, Canada and Senior Research Fellow at De Montfort University).

MEDIEVAL ENGLAND

The Pre-Reformation Church in England 1400–1530 (Second edition)
Christopher Harper-Bill   0 582 28989 0

Lancastrians and Yorkists: The Wars of the Roses
David R Cook   0 582 35384 X

TUDOR ENGLAND

Henry VII (Third edition)
Roger Lockyer & Andrew Thrush   0 582 20912 9

Henry VIII (Second edition)
M D Palmer   0 582 35437 4

Tudor Rebellions (Fourth edition)
Anthony Fletcher & Diarmaid MacCulloch   0 582 28990 4

The Reign of Mary I (Second edition)
Robert Tittler   0 582 06107 5

Early Tudor Parliaments 1485–1558
Michael A R Graves   0 582 03497 3

The English Reformation 1530–1570
W J Sheils   0 582 35398 X

Elizabethan Parliaments 1559–1601 (Second edition)
Michael A R Graves   0 582 29196 8

England and Europe 1485–1603 (Second edition)
Susan Doran   0 582 28991 2

The Church of England 1570–1640
Andrew Foster   0 582 35574 5

STUART BRITAIN

Social Change and Continuity: England 1550–1750 (Second edition)
Barry Coward   0 582 29442 8

James I (Second edition)
S J Houston
                                                    0 582 20911 0

The English Civil War 1640–1649
Martyn Bennett
                                                    0 582 35392 0

Charles I, 1625–1640
Brian Quintrell
                                                    0 582 00354 7

The English Republic 1649–1660 (Second edition)
Toby Barnard
                                                    0 582 08003 7

Radical Puritans in England 1550–1660
R J Acheson
                                                    0 582 35515 X

The Restoration and the England of Charles II (Second edition)
John Miller
                                                    0 582 29223 9

The Glorious Revolution (Second edition)
John Miller
                                                    0 582 29222 0

EARLY MODERN EUROPE

The Renaissance (Second edition)
Alison Brown
                                                    0 582 30781 3

The Emperor Charles V
Martyn Rady
                                                    0 582 35475 7

French Renaissance Monarchy: Francis I and Henry II (Second edition)
Robert Knecht
                                                    0 582 28707 3

The Protestant Reformation in Europe
Andrew Johnston
                                                    0 582 07020 1

The French Wars of Religion 1559–1598 (Second edition)
Robert Knecht
                                                    0 582 28533 X

Phillip II
Geoffrey Woodward
                                                    0 582 07232 8

The Thirty Years' War
Peter Limm
                                                    0 582 35373 4

Louis XIV
Peter Campbell
                                                    0 582 01770 X

Spain in the Seventeenth Century
Graham Darby
                                                    0 582 07234 4

Peter the Great
William Marshall
                                                    0 582 00355 5

EUROPE 1789–1918

Britain and the French Revolution
Clive Emsley
                                                    0 582 36961 4

Revolution and Terror in France 1789–1795 (Second edition)
D G Wright

0 582 00379 2

Napoleon and Europe
D G Wright

0 582 35457 9

The Abolition of Serfdom in Russia, 1762–1907
David Moon

0 582 29486 X

Nineteenth-Century Russia: Opposition to Autocracy
Derek Offord

0 582 35767 5

The Constitutional Monarchy in France 1814–48
Pamela Pilbeam

0 582 31210 8

The 1848 Revolutions (Second edition)
Peter Jones

0 582 06106 7

The Italian Risorgimento
M Clark

0 582 00353 9

Bismarck & Germany 1862–1890 (Second edition)
D G Williamson

0 582 29321 9

Imperial Germany 1890–1918
Ian Porter, Ian Armour and Roger Lockyer

0 582 03496 5

The Dissolution of the Austro-Hungarian Empire 1867–1918 (Second edition)
John W Mason

0 582 29466 5

Second Empire and Commune: France 1848–1871 (Second edition)
William H C Smith

0 582 28705 7

France 1870–1914 (Second edition)
Robert Gildea

0 582 29221 2

The Scramble for Africa (Second edition)
M E Chamberlain

0 582 36881 2

Late Imperial Russia 1890–1917
John F Hutchinson

0 582 32721 0

The First World War
Stuart Robson

0 582 31556 5

EUROPE SINCE 1918

The Russian Revolution (Second edition)
Anthony Wood

0 582 35559 1

Lenin's Revolution: Russia, 1917–1921
David Marples

0 582 31917 X

Stalin and Stalinism (Second edition)
Martin McCauley

0 582 27658 6

The Weimar Republic (Second edition)
John Hiden

0 582 28706 5

The Inter-War Crisis 1919–1939
Richard Overy

0 582 35379 3

Fascism and the Right in Europe, 1919–1945
Martin Blinkhorn
0 582 07021 X

Spain's Civil War (Second edition)
Harry Browne
0 582 28988 2

The Third Reich (Second edition)
D G Williamson
0 582 20914 5

The Origins of the Second World War (Second edition)
R J Overy
0 582 29085 6

The Second World War in Europe
Paul MacKenzie
0 582 32692 3

The French at War, 1934–1944
Nicholas Atkin
0 582 36899 5

Anti-Semitism before the Holocaust
Albert S Lindemann
0 582 36964 9

The Holocaust: The Third Reich and the Jews
David Engel
0 582 32720 2

Germany from Defeat to Partition, 1945–1963
D G Williamson
0 582 29218 2

The French at War, 1934–1944
Nicholas Atkin
0 582 36899 5

France since the Second World War
Tyler E Stovall
0 582 36882 0

Britain and Europe since 1945
Alex May
0 582 30778 3

Eastern Europe 1945–1969: From Stalinism to Stagnation
Ben Fowkes
0 582 32693 1

Eastern Europe since 1970
Bülent Gökay
0 582 32858 6

The Khrushchev Era, 1953–1964
Martin McCauley
0 582 27776 0

NINETEENTH-CENTURY BRITAIN

Britain before the Reform Acts: Politics and Society 1815–1832
Eric J Evans
0 582 00265 6

Parliamentary Reform in Britain c. 1770–1918
Eric J Evans
0 582 29467 3

Democracy and Reform 1815–1885
D G Wright
0 582 31400 3

Poverty and Poor Law Reform in Nineteenth-Century Britain, 1834–1914:
From Chadwick to Booth
David Englander
0 582 31554 9

The Birth of Industrial Britain: Economic Change, 1750–1850
Kenneth Morgan

0 582 29833 4

Chartism (Third edition)
Edward Royle

0 582 29080 5

Peel and the Conservative Party 1830–1850
Paul Adelman

0 582 35557 5

Gladstone, Disraeli and later Victorian Politics (Third edition)
Paul Adelman

0 582 29322 7

Britain and Ireland: From Home Rule to Independence
Jeremy Smith

0 582 30193 9

TWENTIETH-CENTURY BRITAIN

The Rise of the Labour Party 1880–1945 (Third edition)
Paul Adelman

0 582 29210 7

The Conservative Party and British Politics 1902–1951
Stuart Ball

0 582 08002 9

The Decline of the Liberal Party 1910–1931 (Second edition)
Paul Adelman

0 582 27733 7

The British Women's Suffrage Campaign 1866–1928
Harold L Smith

0 582 29811 3

War & Society in Britain 1899–1948
Rex Pope

0 582 03531 7

The British Economy since 1914: A Study in Decline?
Rex Pope

0 582 30194 7

Unemployment in Britain between the Wars
Stephen Constantine

0 582 35232 0

The Attlee Governments 1945–1951
Kevin Jefferys

0 582 06105 9

The Conservative Governments 1951–1964
Andrew Boxer

0 582 20913 7

Britain under Thatcher
Anthony Seldon and Daniel Collings

0 582 31714 2

INTERNATIONAL HISTORY

The Eastern Question 1774–1923 (Second edition)
A L Macfie

0 582 29195 X

India 1885–1947: The Unmaking of an Empire
Ian Copland

0 582 38173 8

The Origins of the First World War (Second edition)
Gordon Martel

0 582 28697 2

The United States and the First World War
Jennifer D Keene   0 582 35620 2

Anti-Semitism before the Holocaust
Albert S Lindemann   0 582 36964 9

The Origins of the Cold War, 1941–1949 (Second edition)
Martin McCauley   0 582 27659 4

Russia, America and the Cold War, 1949–1991
Martin McCauley   0 582 27936 4

The Arab–Israeli Conflict
Kirsten E Schulze   0 582 31646 4

The United Nations since 1945: Peacekeeping and the Cold War
Norrie MacQueen   0 582 35673 3

Decolonisation: The British Experience since 1945
Nicholas J White   0 582 29087 2

The Korean War
Steven Hugh Lee   0 582 31988 9

The Origins of the Vietnam War
Fredrik Logevall   0 582 31918 8

The Vietnam War
Mitchell Hall   0 582 32859 4

WORLD HISTORY

China in Transformation 1900–1949
Colin Mackerras   0 582 31209 4

Japan faces the World, 1925–1952
Mary L Hanneman   0 582 36898 7

Japan in Transformation, 1952–2000
Jeff Kingston   0 582 41875 5

US HISTORY

American Abolitionists
Stanley Harrold   0 582 35738 1

The American Civil War, 1861–1865
Reid Mitchell   0 582 31973 0

America in the Progressive Era, 1890–1914
Lewis L Gould   0 582 35671 7

The United States and the First World War
Jennifer D Keene   0 582 35620 2

The Truman Years, 1945–1953
Mark S Byrnes   0 582 32904 3

The Korean War
Steven Hugh Lee

0 582 31988 9

The Origins of the Vietnam War
Fredrik Logevall

0 582 31918 8

The Vietnam War
Mitchell Hall

0 582 32859 4